OLD TIMES
in
Contra Costa

FRONTISPIECE: *A picnic in Mitchell Canyon, 1883. As you can see, people got dressed up for picnics in that era. Did you notice the lady with the banjo?*

OLD TIMES
in
Contra Costa

by Robert Daras Tatam

with Emily Tatam, Earl Berkeley, and Paul Anderson

Profusely illustrated

Photographs by F.J. Geisler, A.G. Davies, H. Lancaster, La Perla Studio, Hunt Photographers, Russ Reed, George Derbfus, Paul Anderson, Robert D. Tatam , and many, many others—amateur and professional— whose names have been lost to posterity

Art work by Dickinson Weber, Loicy Myers, Sylvia Rhoades, Thomas A. Dorgan, E. Wyttenback, Robert D. Tatam, several anonymous lithograph artists who worked for Smith & Elliott in the late 1800s, and others whose names we do not have

Highland Publishers
Pittsburg, California

Kids got free elephant rides at the grand opening of the new Purity Store in downtown Concord, It seems like only yesterday, but this picture was taken in 1959. And the author has to admit that his kids, Robin and Bobby Tatam are among those onboard (on the elephant's right; your left).

PREFACE: *This is a New Kind of History Book*

This is a new kind of history book—written for your enjoyment. Each page is a short story in itself, giving you a glimpse of a past way of life—or of a place that no longer exists as it once did. Each page, however, implies more than what you see. For instance, there is a picture of a barber shop in Chapter 3. There were actually many similar barber shops at that time. By learning about this one you get a pretty good idea of what barber shops were like in that era.

This format does have limitations. I have learned more about Contra Costa history than I could possibly tell you about here. I could have written a 1,000-page book, but wanted to create a shorter, less expensive book that would be bought and read by more people. Much of the material in this book is completely original, not to be found in any other book. The research has been intensive and the facts are accurate, as far as I know. If you have any questions, corrections, or comments please write to me in care of the publisher.

As the title indicates, this book is about "old times." Except for incidental explanations, nothing that happened after 1960 is recounted here.

The design of the book was inspired in part by the wonderful *Life* magazines of the 1930s and '40s, but I've broken some rules for book design that I can't blame on *Life*. There are no running heads or footnotes—and you won't find an appendix, bibliography, or index. (Since the book doesn't have an appendix, it will never need an appendectomy.)

On the acknowledgments page you will find a list of people who contributed to this work, but here I want to give credit to Ruth Galindo, Brother Dennis Goodman, Virgie Jones, Louis Stein, Jr., and Charles Weeks, Jr., who each went the second mile. Without them I couldn't have produced this volume.

Because of the brevity of this work, I present the best stories and pictures available. However, there are several pictures and stories I regret having to leave out. Perhaps there will be a sequel.

It is fun to write a book, but it is also hard work. I'm glad it's done. I hope you like it.—*R.D.T., April 1993*

Table of Contents

Copyright © 1993 Robert Daras Tatam

Cataloging In Publication Data
Tatam, Robert Daras 1926 -
1. California history
2. Contra Costa County

Library of Congress Catalog Card No. 93-091634
International Standard Book No. 0-9637954-0-6

Published by **HIGHLAND PUBLISHERS**
Division of Highland Rock City, Incorporated
Ralph W. Burgess, President
1625 Buchanan Road, Pittsburg, California 94565
Telephone (510) 432-0700 or 432-2282

DEDICATION

to Ethel Johnston

and to the memory

of George Johnston

and Lillian and Albert Burgess

all Contra Costa pioneers

in the Twentieth Century

ACKNOWLEDGMENTS: *Many People Contributed Information and Pictures*

You would not be holding this book in your hand right now if it weren't for the enthusiasm and support given by my friend of 27 years, Ralph Burgess. He is the guy who encouraged me and pushed me when I needed it and helped in countless ways to get the project finished. .

This book is a bringing-together of material collected from many sources over a period of some three decades.

Some of the pictures and stories have been published previously in historical calendars sponsored by various local banks, which I designed and wrote in colaboration with my late wife, Emily Tatam, who also taught me much of what I have learned about style. (The first of those calendars was published in 1964, so you might say that I have been working on this book for 29 years.) Emily provided the "feature touch" for some of the stories in Chapters 3, 4, 6, 8, 9, 10, 13, & 15. Some of the material on Concord was contributed by my old friend and one-time business partner, Paul Anderson. My late father-in-law, Earl Berkeley, provided some of the words and phrases in the stories about Antioch and Richmond.

Most of the research materials, including pictures, were close at hand, in my files, but I also used the facilities of several libraries and archives, including several branches of the Contra Costa public library system, the Richmond library, the library at Saint Mary's College, the California State Library in Sacramento, the *Contra Costa Times* library, the archives of Pacific Telephone (now called Pacific Bell), and several other research facilities. I have also made use of the Contra Costa History Center in Pleasant Hill, and history museums in Richmond, Martinez, Walnut Creek, Crockett, and Pittsburg.

My partner, Loicy Myers, helped in many ways during the past two years , a period in which I have done the most intensive work on this project.

The bibliography of books, scholarly theses, unpublished manusripts, newspaper articles, and other material is far too extensive to be given here, but can be provided for a nominal charge upon request. (An index to "Old Times in Conta Costa" may also be compiled if there is sufficient demand.)

Over the years I have interviewed many people: oldtimers and their descendants, public officials, teachers, merchants, and historians. Frankly, I've got so much research material stuffed into file drawers and cardboard boxes that I don't remember where it all came from. However, I do have the names of many people who loaned me photos to copy and/or provided information and/or helped in some other way. They are listed below:

Father Bill Abeloe
Mrs. Tony Accinelli
Marti & Jack Aiello
Vince Aiello
H.L. "Hal" Albertsen
Mr.&Mrs. Edgar Bacon
Charlotte Ballenger
Tom Bates
Larry Battaglin
Ruth Beloof
Barbara Benedict
Irving Berg
Vickie Bertoglio
Mr.&Mrs.Frank M. Billeci
Lila Bladen
Roy S. Bloss
Sen. Daniel Boatwright
Charles A. Bohakel
Grace Bonanno
Gus Borba
Brenda Boswell
Farmer Boyd
Justice A.F. Bray
Andreas Brown
Bill Buchanan
Gail and Ralph Burgess
Alan Burton
Grant Burton
Ann Buscaglia
Eva Buscaglia
Mario Buscaglia
Gina Cacciola
Monte Canciamilla
Vince Caruso
Don Church

George Collier
Bob Conner
Phil Cox
Al deGrassi
John A. DeVito
Bert Davi
Eleanor Davidson
Bill Dietz
Erma Dodson
Gentry Durham
Ruth Dyer
Grace Ellis
Tony Enea
Bob Estes
Michael Evanhoe
Art Evans
Bill Evans
JoAnn Evans
Hart Fairclough
Barbara Ferguson
Lupe Ferguson
William Fereira
Leonora Fink
Albert W. Flaherty
Barbara Fogerson
Lorraine Force
Dolores Foubert
Carmen Frank
Garrett Frank
Segrid Frank
Mrs. Leonard Frazee
Theresa & Harry Freed
Toni Friedman
Ruth Galindo
Harry Gamble

Judge John Garaventa
Thomas F. Gates
Ed Garlick
Traci Gibbons
Gerould Gill
Jennifer H. Gomes
Brother Dennis Goodman
Shirley Green
Robert Gromm
Frank N. Grossman
Guy Harris
Jill Harris
Jim Henderson
Margaret Hernandez
Jack Horton
Eldora Hoyer
Paul Hughey
John Jegi

Sal Jimno
Joan the Bartender
Virgie V. Jones
John F. Jordan
James B. Jory
Mr.&Mrs. Roy Joseph
Ethel Kerns
Rich Kimball
Jackie Koehler
A. Paul Kraintz
Pat Kramer
Chris Lanzafame
Delfo Lanzafame
Richard T. LaPointe
Steve Lawrence
Dean Lesher
Frank Lombardi
Jerry Lombardi
B.L. Lonsdale
Eva Lozano

Larry Lucas
Kay Ludolph
Judy Madeiras
Betty Maffei
Wilmetta Mann
Joseph Mariotti, M.D.
Julie Mattson
Ted Maupin
Janet McEwen
Archie & Marilyn McFaul
William L. McNeil
Shirley Medau
Mario Menesini
Paul Merriam
Joan Merryman
Evelyn Musser
Mary Navarro
Richard Nourse
Genevieve Norton
Elaine Null
Bob & Eileen O'Hara
Patsy Oliver
Jim Olssen
Mary Lou Ortega
Victor Parachini
Jan Parlier
Charlene Perry
Will Perry
Ray Peters
Steve Petker
Kay Reesor
Burton Rice
Jim Ritch
Bill Rosales
Carol & A.W. Robbins

Patrick Robbins
Archie Roberts
Verne Roberts
Verne L. Roberts
Vernon Rouner
Al Sapone
Sylvia Schoegel
Father Paul Schmidt
Shirley Schremp, R.N.
Marvin Scott
Jessica S. Serb
Laverne Setzer
Muir (Sorrick) Shank
Will Sharkey, Jr.
Howard Shelley
Guy Spencer
Louis Stein, Jr.
Edwin Stokes
Gil Swift
Robin Tatam
King Tolles
Bill Tornheim
Andy Traverso
Aldo Vasconi
Peter Vasconi
Rep. Jerome Waldie
Nan Wallace
Dickinson Weber
Charles Weeks, Jr.
Jerry Wentling
Wilma Williams
Mae Williamson
Melvin Williamson
Ida Wilt
Rev. John W.Winkley

Narberes family's Concord French Laundry delivery wagon, , ca. 1915

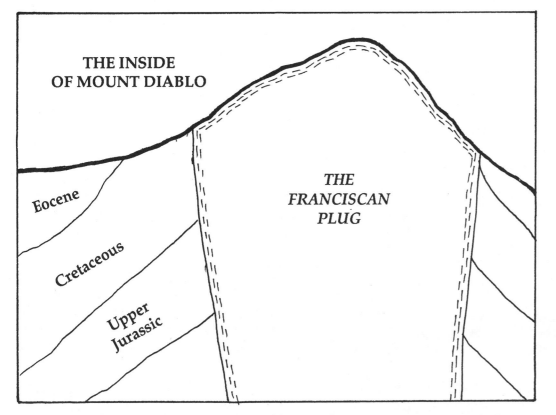

THE INSIDE OF MOUNT DIABLO

Eocene

Cretaceous

Upper Jurassic

THE FRANCISCAN PLUG

TIGERS In Contra Costa?
Strange Primitive Beasts Once Roamed Where Subdivisions Now Flourish

When Mount Diablo Was Under Water
The Mountain Is a "Plug" That Popped Up in the Late Pliocene Age

A "plug" that popped up through the Pacific Ocean, later named Mount Diablo, is part of a group of 155-million-year-old rocks called the Franciscan formation. This formation is composed of sedimentary, igneous, and metamorphic rocks. The sedimentary ocean floor that the Franciscan plug buckled through is six miles thick on the eastern side of the mountain. Scientists think that compressive forces related to the San Andreas fault pushed the mountain up. There are many types of rocks, sea shells, and minerals (including gold, silver, and quicksilver) to be found on the mountain, but the most profitable find was the coal field five miles north of the two peaks, which produced millions of dollars worth of "black diamonds" from 1870-1890.

Smilodon, the saber-toothed tiger, and Megatherium, an elephant-sized ground sloth, were among the beasts that roamed the Contra Costa area for 35 million years, finally dying out during the Pleistocene Age. Later animals included the first deer, Protocera, with horns that sprouted from the nose and above the eyes. Still later there were 18-foot-tall camels, short-legged rhinoceroses, and huge mastodons that thrived here until about 10,000 years ago. And still later, of course, came the animals found by the Mexican and American pioneers--bears, deer, squirrels, rabbits, and other familiar wild animals still seen today.

While the Egyptians Were Building Pyramids The Yokuts and Costanoans Were Living the Good Life

Various aboriginal peoples came to the American continents over a period of some 5,000 years, starting about 8,000 B.C. They crossed over a land bridge which once existed between Asia and North America, where the Aleutian Islands are today. There were three main groups of these people (now called Indians or Native Americans) living in the Contra Costa area: Yokuts in the area south of Mount Diablo, Saklan in Lafayette and Walnut Creek sites, and Costanoan along the shores of the bay.

Since the population was sparse they were able to live off the land. They hunted deer and small animals, fished in rivers, streams, and the bay, ground acorns into meal to make a sort of bread, and had mastered many skills, including cooking, basket weaving, and making of weapons, clothing and jewelry.

The drawing by Loicy Myers shows two Indian women sorting acorns which will later be ground into meal. Women did most of the work at campsites, such as acorn grinding, cooking, and water carrying. Often their children played nearby while they worked. Men did the hunting and fishing.

Unfortunately, the Indians were not immune to diseases brought by European, Mexican, and American settlers. Entire tribes were killed by such diseases as measles, small pox, and scarlet fever. The Indians of Contra Costa were nearly extinct by the 1870s.

Archeologists from the University of California have done much research at tribal campsites, burial grounds, and shell mounds at Richmond, Clayton, Lafayette, and other places, and have learned much about the Indians' cultures and customs.

Spanish Explorers First Came to Contra Costa in 1772

Engaged in a power struggle with England, Spain determined to expand its colonies in North America. In July 1769 Don Gaspar de Portola raised the Spanish flag over a *presidio* in San Diego and on the same day the Franciscan Father Junipero Serra raised a cross on the new Mission San Diego Alcala. Later that year Portola's men discovered San Francisco Bay. The next year saw the founding of a Spanish mission and *presidio* in Monterey. In March 1772 Captain Pedro Fages set out from Monterey with Father Juan Crespi, chaplain and diarist, along with 14 soldiers, a muleteer, and an Indian guide, to explore Northern California. Within a few days they had arrived at Cerrito Creek (now a boundary of Alameda and Contra Costa Counties) where they killed, cooked, and ate a bear. The next day they camped on the shores of San Pablo Bay, where they saw a large whale "disporting itself," and therefore decided that the bay was deep enough for large vessels. They stopped at the shore of Carquinez Strait, skirted the base of Mount Diablo, and then turned back toward Monterey, camping overnight on March 31, 1772, at a spot just north of the present site of Danville. This was

the first European exploration party in Contra Costa. Four years later Captain Juan Bautista de Anza and his lieutenant, Jose Moraga, led another expedition that pretty much retraced the steps of Captain Fages and Father Crespi. Both groups of explorers met Indians along the way and got acquainted by exchanging gifts. At a place on San Pablo Bay that later became Tormey Captain Anza and his men visited an Indian village and were entertained by Indians singing and dancing. The explorers saw many wild animals, including seals and whales in the bay; ducks, geese, cranes, and pelicans along the strait, and antelope, deer, and elk in the valleys. The picture shows members of the Anza expedition observing a herd of elk near the foothills of Mount Diablo. One can only imagine the delight these men must have felt at seeing Contra Costa in its wild state. Several months after the Anza expedition, Lieutenant Moraga led another party of explorers into the Contra Costa area. This was the first expedition to cross the San Joaquin River. Lieutenant Moraga's son, Gabriel, also became an explorer, and his grandson, Joaquin, later owned a large *rancho* in Contra Costa.

Contra Costa Was Teeming with Wild Animals in Pioneer Times

When Mexican and American pioneers first arrived Contra Costa was teeming with wild animals. There were bears in the foothills of Mount Diablo, elk and deer along the waterways, and rabbits and other small game everywhere. This drawing, of elk crossing Carquinez Strait in the 1840s, was made by E. Wyttenback to illustrate William Heath Davis's famous book, "Seventy-five Years in California."

VICTOR CASTRO ADOBE, EL CERRITO, IN 1955

VICENTE MARTINEZ ADOBE, MARTINEZ, IN 1927

ALTAMIRANO ADOBE, ALHAMBRA VALLEY, IN 1955

RANCHO DAYS

By the 1840s nearly all of Contra Costa was owned by a few retired army officers

In 1821 Mexico -- which included the territory of California -- won independence from Spain. The several Mexican governors of California encouraged rapid settlement of the territory by granting large tracts of land to retired army officers and others who would agree to settle on the land, build a home, and raise cattle and/or plant crops.

In Contra Costa Francisco Castro received Rancho San Pablo and Ignacio Martinez received Rancho Pinole, both in 1823. In successive years there were many other grants: Rancho Briones to Felipe Briones; Rancho Acalanes to Candelario Valencia; Rancho Arroyo de las Nuesces y Bolbones to Juana Pacheco; Rancho Monte del Diablo to Salvio Pacheco; Rancho Laguna de los Palos Colorados to Joaquin Moraga; Rancho Las Juntas to William Welch, and other grants given or shared with people whose surnames have become part of California history: Soto, Sepulveda, Estudillo, Berryessa, Amador, Sunol, Baca, Higuera, and Alviso.

The Mexican families built adobe homes and hired local Indians to do most of the physical work: grinding corn, washing clothes, cooking and serving food, tilling fields, and raising stock. Cattle and sheep provided most of the cash incomes of the ranchos, through the sale of hides and tallow.

Only a Few Old Adobes Have Survived

There were many adobe homes built in Contra Costa on the ranchos. Some were one-story ranch houses; others had two stories. Some were furnished primitively, with home-made chairs and tables—and beds made of rude frames covered with hides, but some had furniture, paintings, linens, and gold and silver candlesticks imported from Europe, the Orient, and the eastern U.S. Some of the adobes have been preserved or restored, but most of them are gone. The Salvio Pacheco adobe has been rebuilt as a replica of its former self. (See next page.) The Moraga adobe was a for-lorn ruin when it was acquired and lovingly restored by Katherine Irvine in the 1940s. The Vicente Martinez adobe was a bit run-down when it was purchased in 1955 by Louis Stein Jr. and his associates, who kept it in trust until such time as the National Park Service was able to take it over as part of the John Muir National Historic Site. The adobe home of Fernando Pacheco was renovated by the Contra Costa Horsemen's Association in the 1940s at the instigation of Sheriff John A. Miller. The Victor Castro adobe in El Cerrito was well maintained for about a century only to be destroyed by fire, with just a few walls left standing -- which were then bulldozed to make room for a shopping center. The Altamirano adobe in Alhambra Valley became the home of John Swett, the educator known as the father of the public school system in California. The Berryessa adobe in Martinez was heavily damaged by the earthquake of 1906 and had to be torn down. Dozens of other adobes -- historical treasures -- have been neglected, van-dalized, and destroyed, and are now gone.

The Story of the Salvio Pacheco Adobe

We don't have space in this book to tell the stories of all the Mexican land grants in Contra Costa. Each has its own unique history. However, the story of Salvio Pacheco's adobe and the vast rancho surrounding it will give you an idea of the *Californios'* way of life and of the changes that took place in the county since the Mexican era.

Salvio Pacheco was the son and grandson of Spanish colonists who had lived in California since 1775. He was born in Monterey in 1793. Following family tradition, he joined the Spanish army at age 17, first serving in Monterey, and then in San Francisco, where he met and married Juana Flores.

When Pacheco's enlistment was up he left the army to become part of the new Mexican administration of California, instituted in 1823, after Mexico won independence from Spain. He served in various civil government jobs in San Jose, including two terms as *Alcalde* (mayor). He applied for a land grant in 1828, finally receiving it in 1834. It was located in the wilderness area of Contra Costa, far from his civic duties in San Jose; therefore he sent his 17-year-old son, Fernando, to the property, along with trusted family servants, to mark the boundaries, build a small house, and start raising cattle.

The land grant can be described in terms of present day landmarks as follows: It was bounded on the east by Kirker Pass Road and on the west it included Sun Valley shopping center. The southern boundary went along Lime Ridge and the northern part took in the town of Clyde, much of the naval weapons station, and part of the Avon refinery.

In 1846, when California came under American influence, Don Salvio retired from government service and moved with the rest of his family to the land grant, which he called *Rancho Monte del Diablo*. The name meant "Devil's Willow Thicket," referring to a grove of willows on the north side, thought to be inhabited by mischievous spirits.

The Miranda brothers—contractors from Sonora, Mexico—were hired to build the Pacheco family's new adobe home, with local ranch hands and Indians doing much of the work.

Many items for the adobe were imported from Spain, coming around Cape Horn via schooners to San Francisco, thence by ferry to Pacheco Landing, which was near the rancho. These items included doors, hardware, chandeliers, furniture, oil paintings, and religious statues.

The walls of the home were made of large adobe bricks, manufactured on the site from clay and straw. The bricks were laid over a rock foundation. The upper story, with six bedrooms, was of wood-frame construction.

Next to the adobe was a separate building, containing the Pachecos' kitchen, dining room and servants' quarters. Eventually there were a number of outbuildings, including barns, sheds, and homes for the rancho employees and their families. A bull ring and a dance pavilion were also nearby.

What could be called the first suburban swimming pool was excavated near the adobe, on the west side. It was lined with brick and filled with artesian well water. For modesty's sake the men's and boys' section was separated from the women's and girls' section by a partition.

Don Salvio hosted many celebrations at the adobe, including rodeos, wedding feasts, and birthday parties. Most notable was an annual 10-day fiesta in June, commemorating the anniversary of the land grant.

But most of the year there was much work to be done on the rancho, with men on horseback every day, while the women stayed home to manage the household, supervising the family's many servants.

Religion was important to the pioneers. Padres came from San Jose and Benicia to say mass at the adobe and to officiate at weddings, baptisms, and funerals.

California became a state in 1850. After several years of routine court procedures, Don Salvio's original title to his land was recognized by the United States government.

During the 1850s and '60s Don Salvio sold much of his land to newly arrived American settlers (some of them being disappointed gold seekers). The newcomers started huge wheat farms, which, because of their greater profitability, gradually replaced the cattle ranches of Contra Costa.

The town of Pacheco, which had been started in 1853 at the site of Pacheco Landing, became an important wheat

Fernando Pacheco

shipping center. However, in the 1860s the town was devastated by a series of floods and many people were driven from their homes and businesses.

In 1868 Don Salvio—with his son Fernando and his son-in-law Francisco Galindo—founded a new town near the adobe. Many town lots were given to the flood refugees. The new town, first called Todos Santos, soon became known as Concord.

Starting with a general store, a machine shop, a hardware store, a millinery shop, and a saloon, Concord grew slowly.

Don Salvio died in 1876, leaving the adobe to his son Salvador. Various members of the Pacheco family lived in the adobe until the 1930s, when it was sold and rented out to a succession of tenants.

Concord had been incorporated as a city in 1905, but continued in fact to be a small, charming country town all through the first half of this century. The most notable change was that the wheat farms became orchards and vineyards, watered by irrigation canals, with a few chicken ranches and dairy farms intermixed.

After World War II Concord began to grow rapidly, with the orchards and farms giving way to subdivisions. The adobe was remodeled by Victor Lavagnino and his partners to become a popular restaurant called Casa Adobe. Under various owners the restaurant continued into the 1970s as the City of Concord spread out over Don Salvio's old land grant.

In 1977 the new Fidelity National Bank which had acquired the Salvio Pacheco adobe, converted it into banking offices.

The building was changed quite a bit—virtually rebuilt. Three of the original adobe walls and six of the original handmade beams were retained in the new structure, which was designed to resemble the old adobe as much as possible. The tiles used for the floor of the bank and the courtyard were reproduced from an old Spanish mission pattern. Decorative tiles were imported from Mexico for a fountain.

Inside the building, at one end, the plaster was removed from a portion of a wall to display some of the original adobe bricks for public viewing. The furniture and decor of the interior were chosen to be in keeping with the adobe's Early California tradition.

As one of the strongest links with history, the big ancient pepper trees that were planted by the Pacheco family still stand in the courtyard, offering their beauty and shade to every visitor.

ABOVE: *The Salvio Pacheco was already 35 or 40 years old when this photograph was taken in the 1880s. At that time the adobe walls were covered with wood siding and there was a wooden-frame-constructed addition on the south side (left) of the original adobe. Notice the barn and other outbuildings on the right. Salvador Pacheco (Don Salvio's son) and his family are standing in front of the adobe with two of their horses.*

RIGHT: *The Casa Adobe was "the" place to go out for dinner or to hold a wedding reception in 1953, when this picture was taken. The adobe had been a home to several generations of the Pacheco family and other tenants before being remodeled to become a restaurant in 1946.*

7

The Stone House: Money, Romance, and Tragedy

John Marsh was the descendant of an Englishman who settled inMassachusetts in 1633, one of the first colonists in the New World. Marsh was a Harvard graduate, an Indian agent, a licensed physician, a wilderness scout and a rancher

He was the first American to live in Contra Costa--and the only American living here for 10 years. Following graduation from Harvard he came to a military post in Wisconsin as a school teacher and medical practitioner. He became an Indian agent; fell in love with and married a French-Indian woman who bore him a son and then tragically died a few years later. Leaving his son with friends, Marsh came west; first to Los Angeles, where he became the first licensed physician in California.

Coming north in 1836 he met Jose Noriega, who had recently acquired the Los Meganos land grant along the San Joaquin River, measuring about 10 by 12 miles. Doctor Marsh bought this land from Noriega in 1837 for $500. This ranch, at the eastern end of Contra Costa, included what is now the city of Brentwood.

Marsh lived in an adobe house, with his many books shelved all around the walls. He hired local Indians as ranch hands to take care of his orchards and vineyards, and to tend his huge herd of cattle. His medical practice extended all over California. John Sutter in Sacramento, Robert Livermore in Mission San Jose, and General Mariano Vallejo in Sonoma were among his patients. Doctor Marsh prospered. He wrote many letters to friends back east encouraging Americans to settle in California. In 1851 he met Abby Tuck, a Santa Clara school teacher, who had been visiting friends in Antioch. It was love at first sight. They were married in a few weeks. In March 1852 a daughter, Alice, was born to the couple. The doctor built a mansion for his family, shown in the photo. It was designed by San Francisco architect Thomas Boyd and built of stone quarried from nearby hills. A 65-foot-high tower was a distinctive feaure of the 16-room house. The house was completed in 1856, but Abby had died just months before. The grieving doctor's own life would soon also end in tragedy; however in his last few months he had the happiness of being reunited with his son Charles, who had come from Wisconsin to see him. On September 24, 1856, Doctor Marsh was killed in Martinez by three disgruntled employees.

Charles Marsh helped track down the killers and bring them to justice. He lived in the stone mansion for awhile. He later became justice of the peace in Antioch.

Alice Marsh grew up to be a beautiful young woman. She married W.W. Camron, grandson of John Marsh's old friend from Wisconsin, Rev. John Cameron. (The grandson spelled his last name differently.)

At one time Alice and W.W. Camron owned land near Mount Diablo (which much later was occupied by the Diablo Country Club). The couple moved to Oakland and built a home which later was used as the Oakland museum. The Camrons helped found Orinda, lost a lot of money in real estate, and got divorced in 1895.

The great stone mansion was occupied for awhile by a succession of caretakers. It came into county ownership years ago and has stood vacant in the open countryside near Brentwood. This writer and friends visited the mansion with county permission around 1980. The windows were boarded up; it was dank and dark inside (we had to use flashlights); the floor was deep with pigeon droppings. Once the county had a plan to repair the historic home (for $3 milion), but nothing has been done.

John Marsh

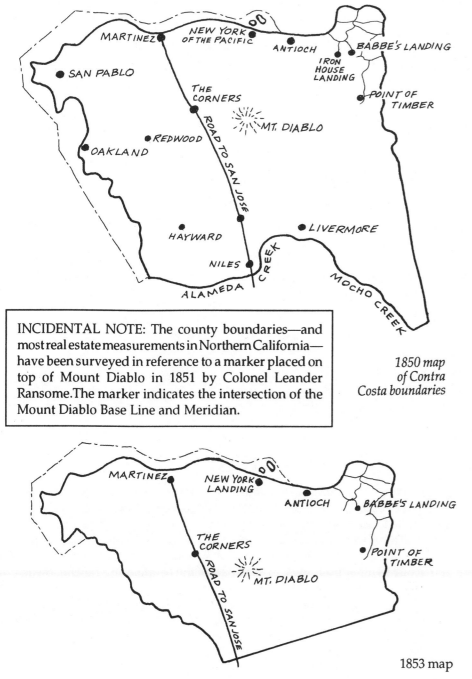

*1850 map
of Contra
Costa boundaries*

1853 map

Founding
Of the County

The late 1840s and early 1850s were times of hectic change in California. In 1846 a group of Americans captured General Mariano Vallejo in Sonoma and proclaimed the California Republic. A flag designed for the new nation featured a bear and a star, much like the state flag of today.

The republic lasted only a few weeks. A war had broken out between the United States and Mexico, sparked by a Texas boundary dispute. California soon came under U.S. control, and then after the war California was ceded by Mexico to the U.S. as part of the settlement. Anticipating statehood, which came in 1850, a state constitution was adopted at an election held on November 13, 1849. The constitution provided that the state be divided into counties. In conformance with this provision the first state legislature passed an act creating 27 counties on February 18, 1850. Contra Costa was one of those original counties.

The present 58 counties of California have been formed from subsequent subdivisions of the original 27. The original shape of Contra Costa County is shown in the sketch map above. In 1852 the eastern boundary had a minor change and in 1853 Alameda County was formed out of parts of Contra Costa and Santa Clara Counties. The lower sketch map shows the final boundaries of Contra Costa.

Meanwhile, in 1848, gold had been discovered at Sutter's Mill in Coloma. The news spread rapidly. Would-be miners rushed to California from all over the world in hopes of getting rich. Many of the early settlers of Contra Costa were gold seekers. Some stopped here on the way to the mines and never left; others came back from panning gold to settle here.

The settlers started ranches and towns on land that had been owned by Mexican grantees, usually buying it, but sometimes just taking adverse possession, proclaiming a somewhat dubious doctrine of "squatters' rights." Some unscrupulous Americans—the lawyer Horace Carpentier being a notable example—contrived to virtually steal land by legal and illegal schemes, thus precipitating some disputes over titles that dragged through courts for several generations, with the grandsons and granddaughters of the original litigants finally receiving their due. Dozens of lawyers got rich representing the various claimants.

Chapter 2

Martinez Was Founded in 1849, Before the County Started

The grantee of Rancho Pinole, Ygnacio Martinez, Comandante of the Presidio in San Francisco and later a civil officer in San Jose, moved his family to the rancho after he retired in 1836. His vaqueros had already been working on the rancho, tending large herds of cattle, which roamed across the rolling hills. In 1848 Don Ygnacio died. His son, Vicente Martinez, inherited the portion of the rancho which became the original townsite of Martinez.

Dr. Robert Semple had started a ferry service in 1847 from the future townsite, across Carquinez Strait to Benicia. The ferryboats transported thousands of head of livestock to pastures in the north. Later, during the Gold Rush, the same boats helped thousands of miners get across the strait on their way to the Mother Lode.

In 1849 Colonel William Smith, son-in-law of the late Don Ygnacio, saw an opportunity. He persuaded Don Vicente and other rancho heirs to authorize him to start a town in the area around the ferry landing, which was named Martinez. He hired Thomas Brown, son of Contra Costa pioneer Elam Brown, to survey and lay out the town. People came from San Francisco and elsewhere to buy lots.

In 1850 Martinez became the county seat of the newly established Contra Costa County. At that time the town consisted of three stores, a blacksmith shop, a hotel, and about 15 other buildings. In 1851 part of the neighboring rancho, owned by the Welch family, was added to the town.

The Gold Rush subsided, but there were golden fields of wheat raised by American farmers in the countryside around Martinez. By the 1860s the town had become a shipping center for this wheat. For the next 20 years three-masted schooners were often seen anchored off the Martinez shoreline, ready to take on cargos of wheat. The photo shows such a scene.

10

Seeley Bennett's Livery Stable in 1865

One of the busiest places in Martinez was Seeley J. Bennett's livery stable. One could rent a horse and carriage here or board one of Bennett's stage coaches to surrounding towns or to the top of Mount Diablo. Some of Mr. Bennett's customers and employees posed for this photo in 1865. You can get an idea of what transportation was like in that era, when horsepower was provided by real horses. The stable was located at Ferry and Escobar Streets. A few years after this photo was taken Mr. Bennett rebuilt the stable with a meeting hall on top, which was used by lodges and community groups for meetings and parties.

Martinez Fishermen Caught Salmon in the Rivers and Strait

Starting in the 1870s Martinez was headquarters for a salmon fishing fleet. Most of the fishermen were Italian immigrants. By 1882 the *Contra Costa Gazette* reported that there were 250 fishing boats in Carquinez Strait. A fisherman posed with his two daughters for photographer F.J. Geisler on the Ferry Street wharf around 1900. It may have been a Sunday afternoon, because there wasn't much activity on the wharf. Fishing nets were spread out to dry. One fisherman was making repairs on the nets. Several men seemed to be out for a stroll along the wharf; an ocean-going schooner was anchored in the strait. There were three salmon runs each year. The winter run started in January; the spring run in March, and the fall run in August. During each run the salmon remained a short time in the strait, and then began to ascend the rivers. The first catch would be made in the strait; the following day the salmon would have reached Collinsville, and the next day they would be found at Rio Vista. The fish lessened their speed as they got farther up the rivers. Most of the fishermen and their families lived in an area near Grangers' Wharf and Alhambra Creek. One of the babies born in this district in 1914 was Joe DiMaggio, who grew up to become a baseball hero.

Fish Canneries Shipped Thousands of Tons of Salmon

Two salmon canneries started in Martinez in 1882—the Martinez Packing Company and Joseph Black's Cannery. Each firm employed 60 to 100 people during the packing seasons. The cannery workers came from many different ethnic back-grounds, including Mexican, Chinese, and various European nationalities. Some of the Chinese workers are shown just getting off work after the usual 10-hour shift. Before the packing season began many of the workers were kept busy at the canneries manufacturing cans. When the catch started coming in the pace of activity increased. This is a brief description of how the canneries operated:

the fish arrived, having been deprived of heads, tails, and insides by the fishermen. At the canneries they were rinsed and cut into requisite lengths for filling the cans. After the cans were filled and salt added, tops were soldered on. The cans were tested, repaired if necessary, and then moved to retorts where they were cooked by compressed steam. Afterward the cans were coated with lacquer and the labels applied. Many thousands of cans were shipped daily from Martinez to New York, Chicago, Galveston, and other large U.S. cities and to ports in Australia and Europe.

Courthouses of Contra Costa

After the county was formed in 1850 F.M. Warmcastle was elected judge of the court of sessions, replacing Alcalde Elam Brown. Court trials were held in private homes at first because there was no courthouse (or any other public building, except for a jail). In 1854 a two-story brick courthouse was built on Court Street, Martinez. It had a small bell tower on top. The bell was used to call court to session. The courthouse is shown above as it appeared in 1890, amid a small park with curving paths. County government outgrew the original courthouse and it was replaced in 1901 by the building shown at right, located at Pine and Escobar Streets. This Greco-Roman structure served as the county's only big office and courts building until 1933, when the Hall of Records was built. In 1954 the supervisors were worried about the cupola falling through the roof of the courthouse if there were an earthquake and ordered the cupola removed. When the contractor got started on the job in July 1956 it was found that the sheet-iron cupola was quite sturdy and that the fears were unjustified. However, since he had a contract to remove it, the contractor went ahead with the job, taking the cupola apart piece by piece. The job took until March 1957. In 1964 a 12-story county administration building was completed, initiating the movement of various county departments. In 1966 the courts and the designation "courthouse" were shifted to the Hall of Records and the building in the photo became the Public Finance Building.

John Muir's Home Overlooked a Serene Valley

John Muir, Contra Costa's most famous resident, lived in the big Victorian home shown below, surrounded by an 840-acre farm. One of his neighbors was John Swett, known as the father of the public school system in California. This photo was taken by F.J. Geisler in 1910 from the Santa Fe railroad trestle. Mr. Muir liked to meditate in the small bell tower on top of the house. He wrote most of his books in a paper-strewn study on the second floor.

A native of Scotland, 10-year old Johnny Muir migrated with his family to the Wisconsin frontier. He worked on his father's farm, clearing trees, planting crops, and building barns. He attended the University of Wisconsin for several years and then started a life-long study of nature, becoming an authority on glaciers and wilderness lands.

After coming to California he married the daughter of Dr. John Strentzel, an Alhambra Valley orchardist. The Victorian home in the photo originally belonged to Dr. Strentzell. The Muir family moved in after the death of the doctor in 1890.

Muir had made a lot of money as an orchardist and, from the 1890s onward, was able to devote all of his time to traveling and writing. His books and magazine articles led to the creation of the National Park System.

He was a founder and first president of the Sierra Club and a friend and adviser to U.S. President Theodore Roosevelt. For his accomplishments in the field of conservation Mr. Muir was honored on a U.S. postage stamp, shown at right. His home is now a National Historic Site, open to the public

Martinez Bottling Plant Made Sarsaparilla and Root Beer

After operating a boarding house in Nortonville during the 1870s, Martin Bonzagni moved in 1882 to Pacheco, where he operated the Excelsior Soda Works. The company manufactured and bottled sarsaparilla, root beer, and other soft drinks. Within a few years Excelsior Soda Works moved to Martinez, where there were more customers. The photo shows Mr. Bonzagni at the reins of his delivery wagon, in front of his Martinez plant. An employee is loading a crate of soda water onto the wagon. Louis Bonzagni, son of the proprietor, is standing in the doorway. Another son, Achilles, also worked in the business, but is not shown in this picture.

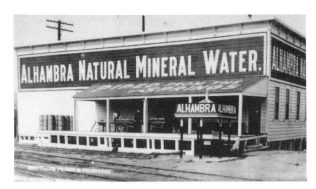

World-Famed Alhambra Water Was First Bottled in Martinez

Loron Lassell was a general store proprietor who also owned a 300-acre ranch in the Alhambra Valley. Using a divining stick he discovered fresh water springs on the ranch. He bottled the water, starting in 1902, and delivered it to homes in San Francisco, Oakland, and various towns in Contra Costa County with a fleet of 33 trucks. The photo shows the Alhambra bottling plant in Martinez in the early 1900s. The water was piped from the springs eight miles away through a two-inch pipeline. The springs were abandoned in 1954 when the Lassell family sold the company to Foremost-McKesson. Now you can buy Alhambra Water in stores everywhere, but it's not the same water that once gushed forth from the Lassell family's springs.

Christian Brothers Wineries Started in Martinez

In 1879 the estate of Henry Bush sold 70 acres of land near Brown Street in Martinez to the Christian Brothers, who started a novitiate on the property to educate future teachers in Catholic schools and colleges. Grape vines had already been planted by Mr. Bush on 12 acres of this land. In 1882 the brothers started crushing the grapes to make sacramental wines, and then started making wines commercially to help finance the novitiate. This was the beginning of the great Christian Brothers wineries, which moved to the Napa Valley in 1932 to expand their vineyards and wine-making facilities. The novitiate in Martinez is shown as it appeared in 1910.

Granger's Wharf Was Built for Shipping Wheat; It Was Later Used as a Fishing Boat Dock

Grangers' Wharf gave farmers direct access to U.S. and foreign markets, thus saving commissions formerly paid to brokers. The wharf was built by the Grangers' Warehousing and Business Association, which had been started at a combined meeting of the Danville, Walnut Creek, and Alhambra Granges held at Walnut Creek on June 1, 1875. The 1,900-foot wharf, a roadway to it, and the first of two warehouses were completed in 1876. The first shipment of wheat left Grangers' Wharf aboard a ship bound for Liverpool, starting two decades of bustling activity, in which many millions of tons of wheat were shipped from Martinez. This activity came to an end in the 1890s, as world wheat prices went into a downward spiral. No longer used for world shipping, the wharf became a place for fishing boats to tie up, as shown in this picture, which was taken around the turn of the century.

A Placid Farm Scene Along Franklin Canyon Road

As president of the Alhambra Grange, Dr. John Strentzel had warned that wheat would become less profitable as the years went by. He called for diversification of crops and advised farmers to plant orchards and vineyards on part of their acreage. "Reap the profits from fruit, raisins, and wine," he said. Farmers all over Contra Costa followed this advice and the golden wheat fields gradually disappeared. The photo shows the Zuppan ranch, which occupied a quarter-section just off Franklin Canyon Road, with a field of corn out in front, and tomatoes and other row crops near the farmhouse, along with a family orchard and vineyard. As you can see, this was a time when clothes were dried out in the sunshine rather than in energy-wasting appliances.

Mountain Copper Company, manufacturers of MoCoCo Fertilizers. You can see Carquinez Strait and Solano County hills in the background.

Industrial Firms Found Sites near Martinez

In 1895 Union Oil Company purchased land near Rodeo for a refinery. This was the first major industrial giant to locate in the Martinez area. The next one was Bull's Head Oil Company, which started an oil refinery near the eastern edge of Martinez in 1904, followed by the Peyton Chemical Company, which built a plant a little farther east on hills overlooking Suisun Bay. About this same time Mountain Copper Company erected a smelter on Bull's Head Point. In the next decade—in 1913—Associated Oil Company Company started a refinery at Avon, about three miles east of Martinez, and—in 1916—Royal Dutch Shell began operating its refinery in Martinez. The new industries set off a housing boom in Martinez, with residential developments going up in Mountain View, Martinez Point Tract, and the Homestead Tract. Shell built houses for its management people on the hills above Escobar Street and on Brown Street. Shell expanded its refinery over the years and it became both a source of employment for Martinez residents and a major cause of air pollution, creating a stench that caused many people to refer to the plant as "stinky Shell." The photos show two of the local industrial plants in their early days. Of the entire group Shell turned out to be the most insensitive to environmental concerns, having been fined frequently over the past 70 years for such offenses as contaminating ground water, dumping crude oil into Carquinez Strait (which ruined 100 acres of marsh land along Suisun Bay), and negligently causing many fires and other avoidable accidents. A lawyer who won a suit against Shell after battling the corporation for 10 years stated, "Someone must stand up to stop corporate abuse of the public trust."

Royal Dutch Shell—office building, parking lot, and part of refinery complex

18

Fourth of July Parade Featured *Float of States*

Here come Uncle Sam (Vincent Hoey) and an early day, unofficial Miss California (Lucile Peck) on the Float of States, one of the big attractions at the Martinez Fourth of July parade in 1910. Forty-eight little girls wearing white dresses with blue scarves were seated on the pyramid-shaped float, representing the various states. Dorothy Bristow and Roma McKenzie were maids of honor on the float, which was drawn by four grey horses. Following behind was the Benicia band and then a contingent of veterans of the Spanish War and then the Native Sons '49er float, with Joe Baker dressed like a miner. The *Contra Costa Gazette* estimated that 4,000 people came from all over the county and from San Francisco and Oakland by horse and carriage, train, and on foot to see the parade. The whole town was decorated with flags and bunting for the event, which was planned by a committee which included J. J. McNamara, W. R. Sharkey, C. C. Brown, W.W. Moore, C. H. Hayden, J. H. Morrow, Lucien Baer, Patrick Lucey, F.W. Johnson, and Sam Hoffman. The Eagles, Redmen, and Woodmen lodges each had a float in the parade. There was a float shaped like a boat, with fishermen aboard casting nets and rowing. There was a Fire Queen float with Emma Krimer dressed provocatively in red, followed by the Martinez fire department. Union Oil Company had a float with a miniature oil well apparently pumping crude oil. Many local businesses presented floats, and there were many more bands and marchers and a group of "horribles" and much more than can be described here.

New City Hall Was Built in 1912

It was a festive occasion when the cornerstone was laid for the new Martinez city hall on April 13, 1912, "the proudest day in municipal history," according to a writer for the *Martinez Daily Standard*. The ceremony, pictured at right, was held at 2 p.m. and began with two selections by the Martinez Cornet Band. Speeches were made by city trustee (councilman) R.H. Ingraham and Mayor J.J. McNamara. Trustee Clinton P. Howard presented the trowel to the mayor, who did the symbolic laying of the stone. Children of the Martinez Grammar School sang two songs. Rev. E. Glandon Davies gave the invocation. Trustee Charles G. Bacon deposited various city records, local newspapers, and other items in a "time capsule" in the cornerstone.

The city hall (shown in the circle) had offices for the city clerk, marshall, constable, and the volunteer fire department. Built in the Classic Greco-Roman style, the city hall had Corinthian columns and high arched windows. This magnificent building was razed and the site converted to a parking lot after the city moved its offices into a remodeled school building on Henrietta Street.

New County Hospital Building Completed, 1914

The County Hospital started in 1880 when the Board of Supervisors purchased 13 acres for $825 on a hillside just south of Martinez. Three one-story buildings were built on that site, with the county physician in residence to provide medical care for the indigent, mostly aged former coal miners at that time.

In 1910 the three-story brick building at right in the photo, costing $40 thousand, was built, and in 1914 the nearly identical building at left was added, connected to the first building by an enclosed breezeway. The photo was taken February 28, 1915, by F.J. Geisler shortly after the construction work was finished, but before landscaping work began.

The building at right was torn down in 1962 after an earthquake had weakened it beyond feasible repair.

In earlier times a large vineyard was in front of the hospital, but hospital additions now occupy that area.

Martinez Baseball Club Played in the Three-Cs League

This is the 1923 Martinez baseball team, which played in the "Three-Cs" (Contra Costa County) League along with teams from Concord, Antioch, Crockett, Pittsburg, and Brentwood. The picture was taken by H. Lancaster. We pored over old files of the *Contra Costa Gazette* to learn the players' names (we got only last names in some cases) and to find out how the team did. The men in the back row are (left to right): Soares, first base; Chick Randall, second base; Pinkie Daley, right field; Jimmy Moore, center field; Dutch McNeil, shortstop; McSweeney, right field, and Brigden, third base. Front row: Vanni, left field;, Borba, catcher and captain, Douglas, manager; Hal Dimock, pitcher, and McDonald, utility. The team got off to a slow start in the first half of the season, but took off in the second half, winning five games in a row after the July break, paced by consistent hitting by most of the team and great pitching by left-handed Hal Dimock, probably the best pitcher in the league.

21

In the 1920s Gas Stations and Garages Offered Free Air and Water—and Fast Service

It may be hard to imagine in this day of self-service gas stations, but in the good old days you would drive up to a service station and two or three clean-cut young men would run up to your car. One would offer to "fill'er up," another would check your oil and water, and often a third would check your tires—without being asked. The employees of the Martinez service stations and garage shown in these 1920s photos also added distilled water to your battery, if needed; cleaned your windshield, and said "thank you" when you paid for your gas and oil. The Standard Station (above left) was one of the first to have uniformed attendants. Martin & Rouse (above right), at Alhambra and Green Streets, sold General Gasoline. Jesse Allen's Garage (left), on Pacheco Boulevard, sold Associated Gasoline, made at the nearby Avon refinery. Remember the Flying "A"? There was also a Shell station at Main and Las Juntas Streets.

Solano-Contra Costa Connection

Before 1930 trains going between Contra Costa and Solano Counties had to be carried across Carquinez Strait on huge ferryboats from Port Costa to Benicia. This was the last bottleneck of the transcontinental railroad. To solve the problem a bridge was planned between Martinez and Benicia. Generally recognized as a great engineering feat, the bridge was nearing completion when the photo above was taken in 1930. The crane (center) was used to hoist materials from the barges below. Incidentally, many Martinez people used to fish from the Mountain Copper Company wharf at the right. The bridge was completed on October 15, 1930. It was the longest double-track span in the West. The official opening of the bridge was held on November 1, 1930. Attorney A.F. Bray officiated. The bridge was christened with a bottle of gingerale by Edna Flackus. Among those at the gala event were U.S. Senator Samuel Shortridge, Congressman Frank Buck, Mayor Ramon Claeys, Sheriff R.R. Veale, and Paul Shoup, president of Southern Pacific. A ceremonial crossing was made by the railroad's first locomotive, the *C.P. Huntington*, which had originally been brought around Cape Horn in 1863. It was followed by the *Golden State Number 4408*, the most modern locomotive of the time (behind the *Huntington* in the photo).

Kiwanis Club Had Many Civic Leaders of Martinez

Service clubs have provided fun, fellowship, and a boost to local projects. The Martinez Kiwanis Club included many of the city's leaders and became an example of this kind of organization at its best. Here is a 1932 portrait of the members.

Top row (left to right): Earl McCallum, James Hoey, Fred Wacher, Frank Fogg, John Elmquist, A.B. Wilson, Tom Swift, John Reid, Frank Glass, Harvey Miller, Dr. O.A. Rase, Fred Hittman, and Lorin Johnson.

Next row: Frank Coates, Joe Robrecht, Carl Brann, Howard Jameson, Will Sharkey, and Charles Scott.

Next row: Arthur French, Phil Butcher, Rex Boyer, Eddie Fraga, Dr. J.L. Beard, Dr. I.O. Church, Father Reilly, Charles Bulger, John Finney, Charles Dodge, and Walter Ormsby.

Front row: Roy Davis, Ray Claeys, George Meese, Walter Bartlett, Tom Meehan, Moss Jones, and Harold Williams.

Martinez Main Street in 1939

A photographer took this picture in 1939 standing on the sidewalk in front of the Hook Building on Main Street in Martinez. You are looking east toward Las Juntas Street. The American Trust Company bank stands on the corner. The bank building was errected in 1904 for the First National Bank. It originally had an ornate cupola on top. Across the street was Jameson's Men's Wear, Beard's Jewelry, and Woolworth's. Upstairs in the Hook Building was the Hotel James, named after James Bulger, its first proprietor. On the street level there was the Southern Kitchen Restaurant and McCloud's Newsstand, with newspaper racks out in front. That was where you could buy popcorn for five cents a bag. Behind the photographer, on the left (not shown in the picture) was the Hoffman Cigar Store, which continued for many years. If you were to stand in this same location in 1993 you would see many of the same buildings, but with different tenants.

When It Rained in Martinez—It *Poured*

Martinez has been afflicted by many floods, none of them worse than the flood of 1958. Days of heavy rains combined with high tides and inadequate drainage facilities had caused Alhambra Creek to overflow, covering the entire downtown with several inches of water. The Ward Street bridge slipped into the creek, some roads were blocked by landslides and several families were forced out of their homes by swirling flood waters. Customers had to wade across Main Street with their purchases, as shown in the photo, which was taken April 2, 1958. A bulldozer was used to push mud away from drainage openings, and crews were busy placing sandbags on the street to block the flow. Other areas of the county were also flooded, including Concord, Walnut Creek, and Pleasant Hill. Estimated damaged in Martinez amounted to $450,000; total county-wide damage was at least $5 million.

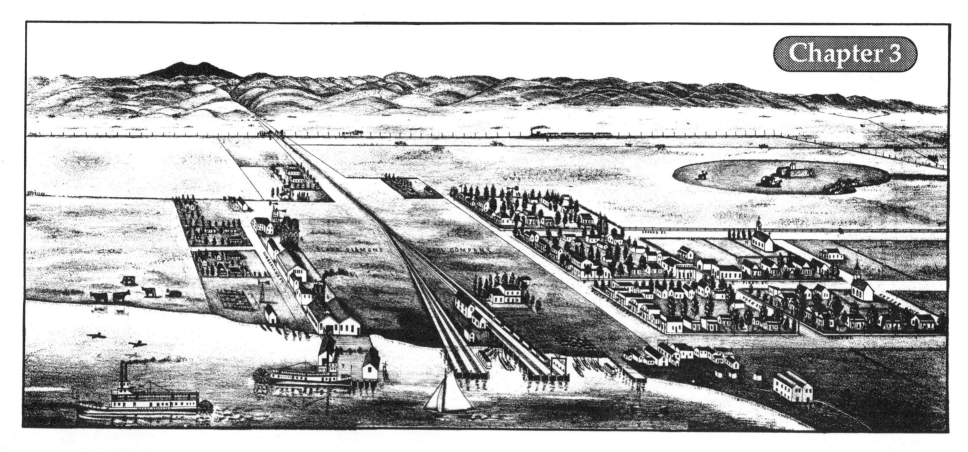

Chapter 3

Colonel Stevenson's Dream--"New York of the Pacific"

Col. Jonathan Drake Stevenson

Colonel Jonathan Drake Stevenson was secretary to Daniel Thompkins, vice president in James Monroe's administration. Col. Stevenson later helped elect Andrew Jackson to the presidency. He organized a regiment during the Mexican War and set sail from New York in 1846 with nearly 1,000 soldiers. Stevenson's Regiment (as it was named by historians) protected California until the peace treaty of 1848. The regiment was disbanded and the colonel decided to settle in California. In 1849 he purchased Rancho Los Medanos (about 10,000 acres) which had been granted to Jose Antone Mesa and Miguel Jose Garcia in 1839. On this land Colonel Stevenson founded what he expected to become a great metropolis--*New York of the Pacific*. But the town fell far short of his expectations and became known as New York Landing. With the discovery of gold near Sutter's Fort the community became an overnight stopping place for would-be miners on their way to the diggings. Colonel Stevenson hired a young army lieutenant, William Tecumseh Sherman, to survey and subdivide the townsite. (Sherman later went on to fame as a Civil War general.) The town grew rapidly after the discovery of coal in the Mount Diablo foothills, becoming, with Antioch, one of the two major shipping points for the coal, and changed its name to Black Diamond in recognition of the product. The drawing shows the town in the 1890s, with many homes, stores, and various enterprises. The Sacramento River Packers Association cannery is shown at left. The railroad from the coal mines is shown coming from the hills and then traversing what is now Railroad Avenue to its docks.

Pittsburg Fishermen Came from Italy

As tradition tells it, in the early 1870s Peter Aiello was the first immigrant to come to Pittsburg from Isola Della Femmine, Italy. When in San Francisco he heard about the excellent fishing around New York Landing (later called Black Diamond and, still later, Pittsburg). Mr. Aiello came by train, stayed four years, and then went back to Italy for his family—with word of the wonderful fishing.

In a few years there a settlement of Italian fishermen: Pittsburg's fishing industry was born.

By 1882 there were two fish canneries, the Black Diamond and the Pioneer. The fishing industry grew and prospered for some 50 years. During most of that time there were more than a thousand men actively engaged in fishing the waters of the Delta region.

The upper photo, probably taken in the early 1930s, shows diver nets and buoys for shad, laid out to dry at the Pittsburg waterfront near the Johns-Manville docks. The concrete building just behind the water tower in the left background was a sardine cannery, the largest in the

world, operated by Frank E. Booth. If you look closely you can see the mechanical conveyor which was used to bring the catch up from the docks. The little building at left—with the smoking chimney—was used for brewing a tanning solution, used as a preservative for the fishing nets.

The fishermen wove their own nets by hand with large wooden needles. Sometimes a man would make a tasseled handbag for his wife out of the same hemp the nets were made of.

The lower photo shows a group of fishing boats at the Paladin Fish Company docks in 1919. Notice the net racks, the cannery buildings, and the houses on First Street in the backround. Boats with little motors were already displacing boats with lateen sails in 1919.

One of the memorable people on the waterfront in that era was August Nunziato, a chandler, who sold rope, tackle, groceries, etc. to the fishermen from a wagon. The fishermen would pay him at the end of the season.

Bowers Rubber Employees Picnicked on the River in 1908

BOWERS RUBBER WORKS employees had a great summer picnic in 1908. They chartered the *Caroline*, a river steamer, and were crowding aboard her for a day of cruising, games, dancing, box lunches, and socializing when this picture was taken. Alfred E. Dunn, superintendent of the hose-making department, and his wife (wearing the white hat) are seated with their daughter, Mrs. Ruth Viera, above the bicycle near the center of the picture. The picnickers sailed up the river to the old Walnut Grove Inn, where they concluded the day's activities with dinner and the prospect of a comfortable sleepy trip back. Early settlers depended on the river for recreation, transportation, and its liberal catch of fish. Because it was a natural deepwater route to the ocean and furnished a good supply of fresh water, the river attracted many major industries to the Delta area.

Bowers Rubber was the second major manufacturer to locate in Pittsburg. C.A. Hooper started the first plant, Redwood Manufacturers, in 1903. Bowers came in 1906 and later merged with H.K. Porter Company. The firm made heavy-duty industrial hoses and fittings. Columbia Steel (U.S. Steel), Great Western Electro-Chemical (now Dow), Johns-Manville, and Shell Chemical all established plants in Pittsburg a few years later.

McFaul's Installed Plumbing and Sold Furniture

ARCHIE McFAUL, SR., came to Black Diamond (later called Pittsburg) in late 1904 to work as a foreman at Redwood Manufacturers. In 1907 he got into the plumbing business with a partner, C.H. Powell. About that same time Archie's father, James R. McFaul, arrived in town from Watsonville and started a furniture store. In 1909 the elder McFaul bought out Powell's interest in the plumbing firm and the two businesses merged under the name J.R. McFaul & Son. This is a picture of the store that same year. It was on Black Diamond Street near First. A huge load of kitchen chairs is being delivered by horse and wagon, with 26-year-old Archie McFaul, Sr., at the reins. The man in the derby hat is J.R. McFaul. An earlier shipment of tables, still in their wrappings, is lined up in front of the building. McFaul's carried all kinds of floor coverings and furniture, including pianos, stoves, and ice boxes. The plumbing division of the firm often had as many as 20 or 30 journeymen out in the field, installing pipe, bathtubs, sinks, etc. in the many houses being built in Pittsburg and Antioch by C.A. Hooper Company and others. In 1907 J.R. McFaul had served as one of the early members of the city board trustees (later called the city council) and his son, Archie, also was elected to the board in 1918, serving for 16 years, 6 of them as mayor. The McFaul store moved to Railroad Avenue, near 6th Street, in 1920. After 59 years at that location it moved again, way out Railroad Avenue, to its present location. For many years it has been run by a third generation owner, Archie McFaul, Jr., and has specialized in housewares.

Jack London's Waterfront Hangout

JACK LONDON is said to have visited the Pittsburg Cafe many times between 1909 and 1914. He would anchor his sloop, *Roamer*, off shore and row in with his crew. He also patronized the Bayview Saloon across the street. Both establishments were at the foot of Black Diamond Street, at Front Street, on the water's edge. The Bayview was on the northwest corner and the Pittsburg Cafe was on the northeast corner. At the time of this picture, about 1912, the Pittsburg Cafe was owned by Frank Fiscus (the man with the "X" on his apron). Shown with him are two patrons and an employee holding a sponge and bucket. Fiscus proudly advertised Yosemite Lager and Steam Beer, both at 5¢ a glass. The place was built in 1905 by Peter Ferrante, who later prospered in the Monterey sardine industry. After Fiscus it was owned by Jack Latimer, father of Annie Latimer Higgins. The Bayview Saloon was operated by David A. Gatto and his brother, Louis. Dave Gatto also ran a barbershop next door. Across from both saloons, on the southwest corner, Jack Junta and Pete McCue had a hardware store and the main business district on Black Diamond Street ran for several blocks southward.

A Busy Day on Black Diamond Street in 1911

THE HUSTLE AND BUSTLE of downtown activities were caught in this remarkable 1911 photograph of the main street in Black Diamond, California, taken just a short time before the 62-year-old settlement was renamed Pittsburg. This is Black Diamond Street, looking south from the First Street intersection, little more than a block from the waterfront, where riverboats brought cargoes from Oakland, Stockton, and up and down the Delta. On the left corner is Senderman & Israel, General Merchandise, just across the street from its chief competitor, Buchanan's, on the right-hand corner. Both stores sold apparel, hardware, and groceries, with free delivery service. Buchanan's also housed the telephone exchange, the Wells Fargo Express office, and the post office. Next to Buchanan's was Keller's Regal Drug Store,

forerunner of the Keller-McDermott chain. Next to Senderman & Israel was J.R. McFaul & Son, plumbing and furniture, followed by James Fitzgerald's real estate and insurance office, then Grabstein Brothers, men's wear and shoes, and Turner & Dahnken's Saloon (they later owned the T & D theatre chain). About the middle of the block on the left side was the Argonaut Hotel, just across the street from its competitor, the Fairmont Hotel, run by J.F. More. As you can see, people walked down the middle of the not-yet-paved street, unafraid of auto traffic, of which there was little. However a few early cars can be seen parked on the street, along with horse-drawn wagons and buggies, one of which can be seen discharging passengers in front of Keller's.

First Airplane to Fly over Bay Area Was Built in Pittsburg in 1911

A historic flight around Mount Tamalpais on December 22, 1911, in a hand-made biplane made front-page news everywhere and thrilled the nation and the world. The flight, first of its kind, began in Oakland. The pilot, Weldon B. Cooke, flew across San Francisco Bay at an altitude of 3,000 feet at 60 miles per hour and then circled the mountain 400 feet above the peak. The airplane was aloft for one hour and twenty minutes. The press called Cooke one of America's foremost and most daring aviators. The plane he flew--*The Diamond*--was built by Captain L.B. Maupin and Bernard Lanteri at Lanteri's Shipyard, at the place where Columbia Steel Works (later U. S. Steel) was built the following year. This photo, taken in the fall of 1911, shows *The Diamond* airplane with (left to right) the pilot, Cooke; a girl friend, Madge Murphy, and the mechanic, Richard Williamson. The plane was also flown by Cooke at a national air meet in Los Angeles, winning both the altitude record and duration-of-flight record with a prize of $700. Several more flights were made and then *The Diamond* was exhibited all over the nation in subsequent years . During an exhibition in 1948 it was badly damaged by propwash from another plane. It was restored and is now at the Smithsonian Institution.

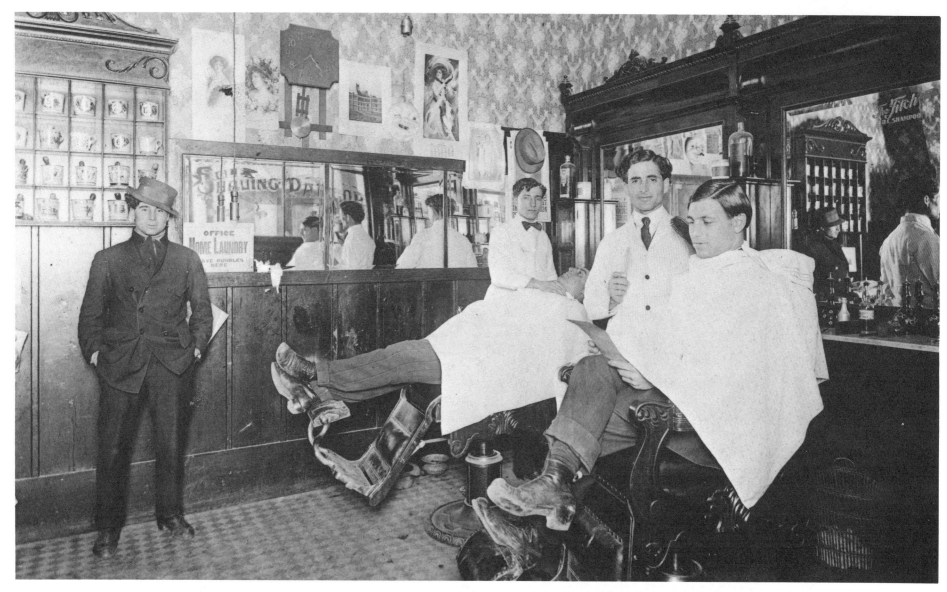

The Eagle Shaving Parlor and Barbershop

THE EAGLE SHAVING PARLOR and Barbershop was located in downtown Pittsburg, on Black Diamond Street, behind the old Waldorf Saloon. The barber in the back, with the bow tie, is Camillo Lanzafame, who later had a long career in the furniture business. He may have been shaving off his customer's "five o'clock shadow," because the wall clock says 4:39. The calendar over the mirror indicates that this picture was taken in February, 1912. It was probably cold outside, as evidenced by the customer at left, with his lapels turned up, Sam Belleci. The proprietor of the shop was Charles Valvo, shown at the first chair holding up a comb and brush—tools of the trade. The shop took in laundry, as you can see by the poster on the mirror. Many regular customers had their own personal shaving mugs, kept on the rack behind Belleci. Before the invention of the safety razor, there were few men able to shave themselves with a straight edge razor, and most went to a barber for their daily shave. Did you notice the 1912 pin-up girls on the wall and the ad for Fitch Shampoo on the mirror?

Pittsburg Had a "BART" Station in 1913

THE OAKLAND, ANTIOCH & EASTERN (later known as the Sacramento Northern) was Contra Costa's first electric "commuter" railway—an ancestor of BART. This is the Pittsburg station, which opened in 1913. The sign, which is not fully visible in this picture, advertised "FAST ELECTRIC TRAINS TO SACRAMENTO, SAN FRANCISCO AND OAKLAND — WOODLAND, MARYSVILLE, COLUSA AND CHICO." In addition to the advertised destinations, travelers could go to many smaller towns along the way, such as Isleton, Walnut Creek, Bay Point (later called Port Chicago), and even down to San Ramon. One of the first automobiles in Pittsburg is parked in front of the station. Note the right-hand steering wheel. The man and woman standing on the platform with their dog are probably the station manager and his wife. As you can see, the electric trains looked something like street cars, with trolleys riding on overhead wires. They were quite elegant, with

arched windows and the name of the railway painted in gold on the side. As the sign in the window indicates, the electric trains carried Wells Fargo Express—the last stage coach run in this area having been made in 1913. All in all it was a fine little railroad. Unfortunately, the popularity of the automobile spelled the end of the line for passenger service. In July 1941, after losing money for years, the pasenger cars were sold off and the line then carried only freight. A few months later the war started, bringing with it gas rationing and tire rationing. Then everybody wished the electric cars were back—but the steel to build them was needed for the war effort. Now, years later, the BART system follows part of the orignal route of the old electric trains. Let it be noted here that BART, with all the millions spent on it, has not yet managed to do something that the small, privately owned Oakland, Antioch & Eastern did: provide rail service from Pittsburg to San Francisco.

The Columbus Day Celebration of 1914

THE 422ND ANNIVERSARY of the discovery of America was observed in Pittsburg on Saturday and Sunday, October 10 and 11, 1914, with one of the biggest celebrations in the town's history. Everybody in Pittsburg came to the various events and excursion trains brought visitors from every direction. The celebration started with a Grand Ball on Saturday night at Pythian Hall, presided over by Mayor F.S. Gregory, who crowned Queen Isabella (Jennie Di Vencenzi of Collinsville) and King Ferdinand (Salvatore Davi of Pittsburg). At 10 Sunday morning the landing of Columbus was re-enacted at Gatto wharf. Columbus was protrayed by Anline Geraldo of Antioch. He is the man standing just to the left of the foremast in the picture above, which was taken just before the landing. The other men in the picture are various civic dignitaries, some dressed up as Spanish sailors. Following the landing a big parade was held, led by the Pittsburg Band. In the afternoon there were sporting events and carnival attractions on the side streets.

Pittsburg Free Market Sold Live Fish and Poultry

THE PITTSBURG FREE MARKET, 139 Black Diamond Street, was started by Leonard Canciamilla and his wife, Carmela, in 1914. This is a picture of the store interior in 1920. The man at left is Joseph Macaluso, a customer, next to another customer whose name is unremembered. Behind the counter are Nick, Monte, and Joe Canciamilla with their father and mother. The girl in the right foreground is Theresa Capurro, another customer. The store sold a full line of groceries, including many items imported from Italy. Did you notice the American and Italian flags displayed in the back? The scale on the left was used for weighing groceries and produce; the one on the right was for fish. The fish were really fresh—customers could pick them out, swimming live in a tank at the front of the store. Poultry also was displayed live, in cages outside. The large machine you see just to the right of Miss Capurro is a coffee grinder. Way up on the back wall, on a high shelf, are some washboards, items you don't see much of anymore. Upstairs from the store was a boxing gymnasium, used by local fighters, including Tony Melrose, Vincent Aiello, and Charles Gallegos. The Pittsburg Free Market moved to 7th and Black Diamond Streets around 1926. The Canciamillas retired in 1936, but then Mr. Canciamilla started a wholesale produce business and didn't retire again until the mid 1950s, when he was nearing 80. The Canciamilla sons all followed different careers.

They Played For Two World's Fairs

THE PITTSBURG BAND has set pulses beating to 4/4 time for three generations. It was formed in 1912, with most of the instruments being imported from Verona, Italy. In 1915 the band was chosen to play at the Panama-Pacific International Exposition in San Francisco, representing Contra Costa County. This is a picture taken that year. Standing (left to right) are Frank Catania, Salvatore Barraco, Victor Giambona, Joe Puccio, Bert Bruno, Orazio Enea, Nick Culcasi, Vincent Costanza, Tony Davi, Steve Cardinale, and Joseph Anello. Seated are Neno DiMaggio, Russel Cataline, Joe DeStefano, Settemo Lucido, Tony Enea, Frank Lucido, and Eddy Barraco. Also in the band, but not in this picture, was Camillo Lanzafame. The original director, Pietro Serafine, quit in 1916 and was replaced by Emillo Civita, who stayed 50 years. In 1939 the Pittsburg Band again represented the county at the world's fair on Treasure Island.

38

Martinez-Benicia Ferryboat Was Built in Pittsburg

THE LAUNCHING of a new ferryboat from the Lanteri Shipyards in Pittsburg was a big occasion on March 6, 1917. Bernard Lanteri, head of the four-year-old firm, had gotten the $60,000 boat built ahead of schedule for the Martinez-Benicia Ferry and Transportation Company. This is a picture taken just a few moments before the launching ceremony. About 3,000 people had come from all parts of Contra Costa and Solano Counties to see it. Standing on the scaffolding, Miss Aileen Sanborn of Benicia cried out, "I Christen thee *City of Martinez!*" as the final blocks were knocked aside and the big new auto ferry glided slowly and easily down the ways. The Pittsburg Grammar School band played stirring martial airs, flags were waved, and a mighty shout came from the crowd as the boat hit the water. Then the waiting tugboats took hold of the vessel and towed her to

the wharves, where the public boarded her for an inspection tour. Later that day the *City of Martinez* was towed to San Francisco for the installation of 250-horsepower steam reciprocating Evans engines. After that, Eureka oil-burning boilers were added and the boat was returned to Pittsburg for painting and mast fittings. She was 167 feet long and 54 feet at beam. She could carry 40 cars and 500 people. On July 2, 1917, she was put into service between Benicia and Martinez, serving for a decade, until the opening of the Carquinez bridge in 1927. The bridge owners had taken over the ferry operation and replaced her with the former Rodeo-Vallejo ferryboat, *Issaquah.* After her retirement, the *City of Martinez* was tied up at the Martinez Municipal Wharf, serving as headquarters for a fishing club until she was destroyed by fire, burned to the waterline, in the mid 1950s.

Onstage at the California Theatre

THE MOLINA FAMILY orchestra was one of the attractions at the California Theatre, Pittsburg, during the 1920s. Originally from Mexico, the Molinas had traveled all over the U.S. with Escalante Brothers carnival until they came to Pittburg. Then they accepted an offer from Sylvester and Salvatore Enea to become the house orchestra at the Eneas' California Theatre. This is a picture of the group onstage around 1925. Most, but not all of them were Molinas. From left to right the people are as follows: bass player, name unremembered; pianist, Tony Enea; violinist, "Artisto" (not a Molina), violinist, "Pipo" Molina; flautist, Professor Molina, father of the other Molinas; conductor, Frank Lucido, who was also theatre manager; clarinetist, Johnny Molina; trumpeter, Joe Molina; trom-bonist, name unremembered, and drummer, Alfonso Molina. The orchestra played onstage when giving concerts and in the pit when playing accompaniment for silent films. The Seeburg Smith pipe organ at lower right was played by Tony Enea, who also gave concerts and played accompaniment to the movies, alternating with the orchestra. The California Theatre had opened in 1920, playing vaudeville attractions along with silent motion pictures. It had 1,000 seats, always filled when top vaudevillians came to town — like Sophie Tucker, Jack Carson, and Edgar Bergen. The California Theatre ceased operation when people started going to newer theatres. Now, as part of Pittsburg's Historic District, it is due for renovation and new use.

40

Landmark Pittsburg Hotel
Was Destroyed by Fire

For some 50 years -- from 1917 through the mid-1940s -- the Hotel Los Medanos rivaled the larger Claremont Hotel in the Berkeley hills as one of the most elegant hosteleries of the East Bay. Famous musicians and singers entertained at the Hotel Los Medanos, especially during the war years, when its bar and restaurant were frequented by soldiers from Camp Stoneman, many of them holding farewell celebrations before going overseas. The hotel was built by C.A. Hooper Company in 1917 for $60,000. It covered a whole block on Cumberland Street, between Eight and Ninth Streets, in Pittsburg. It was an excellent example of California Mission Revival architecture, with arched colonades on three sides of an interior courtyard. The landscaping included palm trees along the street. Every room had hot and cold water, electric lights, telephone, and steam heat. Rooms *en suite* had private baths. All of this was quite innovative in 1917 and for some years after. The lobby had heavy velvet drapes, cane-bottomed chairs, overstuffed couches, oriental rugs, and polished brass spittoons. The hotel hit the skids starting in the mid-1950s and it became more a rooming house than a hotel. On September 28, 1980, the landmark structure was destroyed by a fire that injured four persons, including two firefighters. When the debris was cleared away virtually nothing remained but the neon sign, sitting on top of a metal pole.

Old Pittsburg City Hall Housed
Police and Fire Departments

In January 1920 Pittsburg citizens voted 9 to 1 for a bond issue to build a city hall and to invest in a number of other civic improvements. The city hall served the city well for more than four decades. It was built in 1922 for $75,000 on the north side of Ninth Street, between Railroad Avenue and Cumberland Street. The picture at left was taken in the early 1940s. At that time the city hall housed the fire and police departments as well as the various city offices. The main entrance had a huge archway flanked by massive columns. The city clerk and treasurer were on the main floor, along with the police, finance, water, and building inspection departments. Upstairs were the city council chambers and the city manager's office. The fire department was in the basement, with a ground-floor entrance in the back of the building. There was also a small jail in the basement. At various times in the 1960s the city departments moved one-by-one to the new civic center. And then the old city hall was torn down to make room for the new post office which now occupies the site.

Great Western Electro-Chemical Became Dow

The Great Western Electro-Chemical Company was formed in 1916 by Mortimer Fleischacker, a pioneer in the development of hydroelectric power, and John Bush, former vice president of an eastern chemical company. A plant site in Pittsburg was chosen because of the availability of fresh water, easy access to western markets, and its position near major electric power lines. The plant began making caustic soda and chlorine in July 1916. The company gradually expanded into the manuafacture of other products. This picture, an exceptional example of early aerial photography, shows the Great Western plant in 1925. The odd-shaped building in the lower right hand corner is the Xanthate plant. Xanthate, a chemical used in mining, was patented by H.C. Keller in 1925. The large building at the left of the picture is the cell house. The rectangular building in the center is the old power house. The two small buildings with pitched roofs in the foreground are the research laboratory (left) and the office. The latter is the only building in this picture that is still standing. The road running horizontally at the right middle of the picture is Loveridge Road. In the 1930s the research staff developed a new process for producing chlorinated hydrocarbons, which attracted the favorable attention of Dow Chemical, of Michigan. Dow had been looking for production facilities on the West Coast. After some months of negotiations Great Western merged with Dow in 1939. Since that time the Pittsburg plant has been modernized and expanded several times. Dow has always been conscious of the importance of clean water. In 1974 the firm achieved a long-term goal of completely eliminating waste discharge into the river. Dow has several other facilities in Contra Costa, most notably the lab in Walnut Creek which produced an artificial kidney which has helped prolong the lives of many people.

Steel Mill Ushered in Industrial Era

ONE OF THE MOST dramatic sights in all industry—white-hot metal pours from a gigantic crucible to form ingots. This photo was made in the late 1930s by George Derbfus at the U.S. Steel mill in Pittsburg. At that time the mill produced steel for all sorts of uses—in bars, strips, flat pieces, and tin plate. It also made wire, cable, nails, tacks, springs, and wire netting for fences. The mill was started in 1910 with 60 employees by Charles M. Gunn and originally named Columbia Steel Company. Early steel castings were used in gold dredging, shipbuilding, and the lumber industry. The steel mill was one of the first of many industrial plants to locate in or near Pittsburg. During World War I the mill worked around the clock producing castings for ships being built in West Coast yards. From its inception Columbia Steel was expanded almost annually. By 1923 it covered over 400 acres and had a rod mill, wire and nail mill, and sheet mill. A tin plate mill was added in 1929. In 1930 the plant became the Columbia-Geneva Division of U.S. Steel.

EPILOGUE: *Because of corporate mismanagement, cut-throat competition from Japan, and short-sighted policies of various governmental agencies in the U.S:, the steel mill declined in ensuing years. It came under partial foriegn ownership, paying relatively lower wages to fewer people.*

Downtown Pittsburg in the Late 1930s

RAILROAD AVENUE, from the waterfront to just past Fifth Street, was the main business district of Pittsburg in the late 1930s, when this picture was taken. This is the corner of Fifth and Railroad, looking north. At the foot of the street you can see a boat shed, which later became a picturesque waterfront restaurant. On your left is Buchanan's General Store, which started in 1896 at First and York, moved to First and Black Diamond in 1906, and to the building shown in the picture in 1922. It was operated by William James "Billy" Buchanan and his wife. He served as the first chairman of the Pittsburg board of trustees (a post comparable to mayor) and then as a county supervisor for 42 years. Mrs. Buchanan was postmaster and telephone operator in the town's early years. The site of Buchanan's was later occupied by Klein's Department Store. The Rexall Drug Store, down the street from Buchanan's, filled prescriptions for several generations. The old buildings in this marina segment of Railroad Avenue are being restored to the furbelowed elegance of their Victorian vintage and will recreate for tourists and townfolk an earlier time.

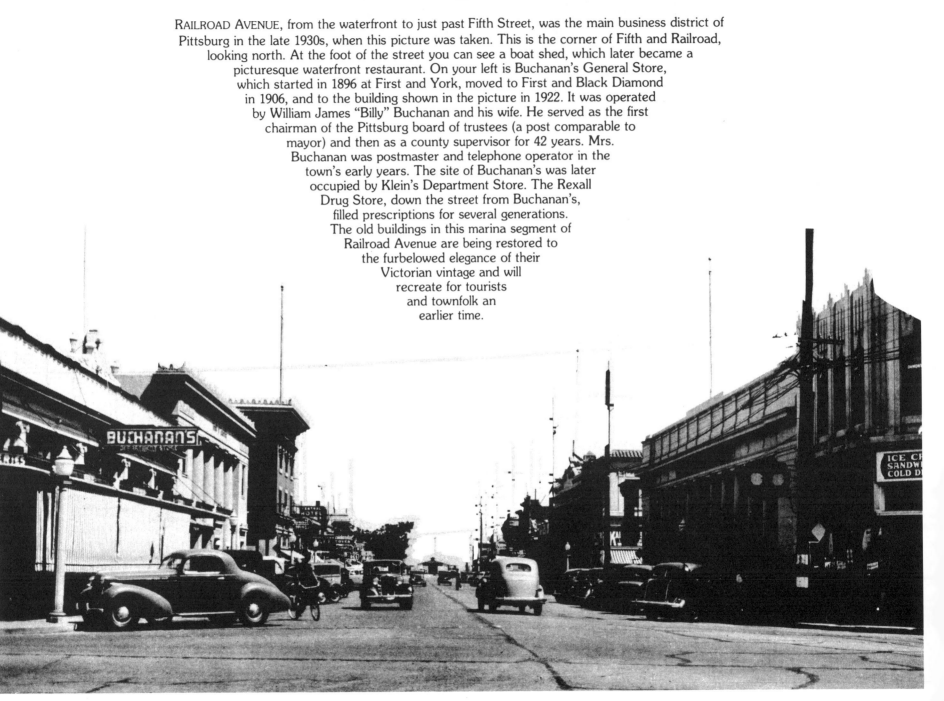

The Grand Columbus Festival Parade of 1947

THE GRAND PARADE up Railroad Avenue, led by a float carrying Queen Isabella and her court, climaxed the five-day Columbus Day Festival in October, 1947. This was the first festival since 1940. The traditional event had been cancelled during the war years. The festival featured many sporting events, including motorboat and hydroplane races, an alumni football game—Pittsburg versus Antioch, a bowling tournament, motorcycle races, and boxing matches. The Pittsburg Municipal Band entertained throughout the festival. One of the most charming features was a children's pet parade. At a Saturday evening dance Miss Rose Continente was crowned Queen Isabella by Mayor Vincent A. Davi. Joseph H. Billeci was master of ceremonies. On Sunday, the last day of the festival, Columbus—portrayed by Gennaro Nuzzo—landed at the waterfront in a seaplane and was welcomed by "Indians" from the Redmen lodge of Concord. This was followed by an air show put on by stunt pilots. Then came the Grand Parade, pictured above heading north at Fifth and Railroad. There were floats and marching and mounted units from all over the state. The Lowry Williams store you see in the picture was torn down a few years later for the new KAL Payless Drug Store building. The brick building on the left was the Coast Counties Gas Company office (now the Post-Dispatch). The palm trees have long since been cut down, the taxi stand moved to a spot behind Lanzafame Furniture, and the Columbus Day Festival is just a memory—the last such event having been held in 1957. It is missed by many.

45

Pittsburg Army Camp: Jumping Off Place to War Zones

CAMP STONEMAN, Pittsburg, was the place where more than a million young men and women said goodbye to America and went off to fight World War II and the Korean War. The Army base was open from 1942 to 1957. It became the largest port of embarkation in the world. In a single month, August 1945, close to 100,000 soldiers were shipped out. During their stay at Stoneman many soldiers were entertained at the Pittsburg U.S.O., which was located in a building on East Street, near Tenth. There were dances, jam sessions, and plenty of good food. Local young women served as hostesses. At Stoneman soldiers were issued weapons, went through combat drills, got medical checkups, and had their teeth filled. Then they went by ferry to Fort Mason, where they boarded ships bound for Pacific Ocean war zones. Fortunately, most of them returned. The photo shows Korean War veterans debarking from a ferry at the Stoneman docks on the Pittsburg waterfront. Camp Stoneman would be their first home in America after their service in Korea.

Old High School Is Fondly Recalled

HERE IS Pittsburg High School about 1947, with a few students relaxing and socializing on the front lawn. The school is fondly remembered by many. Other, newer schools might be bigger or more earthquake-proof, but none will have the charm of that old brick building, which was constructed in 1928. By the time this picture was taken the school could boast an athletic stadium with lights and a spacious cafeteria, both added after the original construction.

The stadium lights were donated to the school by the student body through a loan from leading citizens in 1945, which was paid back in three years. If you were a student at Pittsburg High in the 1940s you might remember lunchtime at Tom's Fountain, at School Street and Railroad Avenue, where you could get a hamburger for 20 cents and play the jukebox for a nickel. And you might remember going on dates to the roller skating rink on 10th Street. There was a little drive-in next door. Later the more deluxe Pirate Drive-In opened on Railroad Avenue. The New Look was the big fashion news of 1947 — with a hemline below the calf, like the dress of the girl at left in the picture. The football heroes of that era — remember them? — were John Henry Johnson, Tommy Hendricks, John Tresta, and Mario Affinito. The old high school building is gone now, torn down in 1953 to make way for a new high school on the same site.

High School, Pittsburg, Calif.

West Pittsburg Was Settled by Wheat and Dairy Ranchers

The first settler in West Pittsburg was Charles N. Wight, who arrived in 1847. He operated a ranch for 40 years at what later became the site of Shell Chemical Company. Mr. Wight was followed by a number of first- and second-generation Americans of Irish, English, Portuguese, and Italian derivation, who raised fields of wheat and operated dairy farms. Among these were several Irish families who arrived in the late 1850s and early 1860s and who acquired adjoining quarter-sections (160 acres each) in what is now the area just east of Bailey Road between Willow Pass Road and the freeway. They paid $1.25 an acre for these lands. These quarter sections were recorded in the names of Henry O'Hara, and his sons John O'Hara, Henry O'Hara, Jr., and George O'Hara, along with John Loftus, George Loftus, James McCloskey, and William Fahey—the latter four being in-laws of the O'Haras. Another O'Hara—James—settled near Oakley, where he became an orchardist. George O'Hara is shown at right in the upper photo, on his farm near Bailey Road and Canal Road, around the turn of the century, with Anton Enes. The complicated wooden contraption they are standing on is a harrow. It had sharp teeth underneath. When it was pulled by horses over the land it broke up clods left by plowing. It was also used to cover sown seeds with earth.

Service Station Was Started by Descendants of Original Farmers

Robert and John O'Hara, sons of the farmer, George O'Hara shown above, got out of the Army in 1945 after their war service and started a service station on the southeast corner of Bailey Road and Willow Pass Road on June 6, 1946. The first customer was Harry Nuttman, the undertaker. Gas was then selling for 19.9 cents a gallon. The station is shown as it looked in 1952. The O'Haras were then selling Flying A gasoline for 32.9 cents a gallon. The Gulf station across the street was undercutting them by one cent, but the O'Hara brothers gave great service and had hundreds of loyal customers. The station continued for 32 years. Bob and John retired and closed the station in 1978, when their lease expired. The road has since been widened by 55 feet and the corner has become the site of a Taco Bell restaurant.

Students at Ambrose School Grew Up to Become Community Leaders

Old Schoolhouse Later Was Converted to a Tavern, and Still Later Became a Church

Here are the pupils and teachers of Ambrose Elementary School in 1923. Two teachers taught all grades from first to eighth. Many of the children pictured here grew up to become professional, business, and civic leaders. Top row (left to right): Peggy O'Neill (teacher), Dorothy Alvarez, Miss Johnson (teacher), Lillian Silveria, Mary Fraga, and Alvin Kennerly. Second row from top: Ida Evora, Doris Kennerly, Delfina Fraga, Mario Rodella, George Wildes, John Faria, Vernon Wildes, and John O'Hara. Third row: Delfina Rodella, Natalie Silveria, Marian Alvarez, Robert O'Hara, Bernard Enes, George O'Hara, Alexander Rodella, and Alvin Faria. Fourth row: Leo Fernandez, Lena Lazzarini, Carmen Seeno, Elsie Lazzarini, Elga Orsi, Geraldine Faria, Ella Mae Kennerly, William O'Hara, and Al Alves. Front row (kneeling): Jack Rodella, Chris Enes, Eugene Alves, Thomas Rodella, Frank J. Seeno, Raymond Faria, Harold Wildes, and Raymond Rodella. The school was built in 1910 on Willow Pass Road in West Pittsburg. A few years after this photo was taken it was replaced by a larger building, also on Willow Pass Road. The former schoolhouse was moved to Canal Road and was used as a tavern, and then was relocated again to North Parkside Drive and became a church. This writer got involved in the history of the building around 1960. As an agent for Lucking Realty I sold the building, then owned by Southern Baptists, to a new congregation and it became the Landmark Missionary Baptist Church.

Ambrose Park Has Meant a Lot to West Pittsburg

Ambrose Park, possibly the most delightful small park in Contra Costa, was established by vote of the people of West Pittsburg in 1946 and was opened in 1948. Its unique terraced hillside barbecue and picnic spots could well be copied by park designers in other communities. Shown above is a poignant moment during a 1952 Memorial Day program. Two Boy Scouts of Ambrose Troop Number 196, Lawrence Durbin (left) and Danny Null, are raising the flag to half-mast to honor members of the armed forces who gave their lives in past wars. The program, which became an annual event, was sponsored by the board of directors of the park district. Guest speaker was Mrs. L.B. McKinnon of Concord, past state president of the American Legion Auxilliary. Rev. Clifford Nixon, Ambrose Community Covenant Church, gave the invocation. Capt. Garret Nalley, chaplain at Camp Stoneman, gave the benediction. A color guard and firing squad also came from the local army camp. Master of ceremonies Bernard Enes introduced Supervisor W.G. Buchanan and members of the park board: Gustave Anuta, Art Franceschi, Alfred Dunn, and Elaine Null. The park has a swimming pool, tennis court, horseshoe pit, softball diamond, and recreation hall.

50

Early Settlers In Antioch Were Seafarers From Maine

The first permanent settlers in Antioch came as a result of a do-it-yourself ship-building project started on the coast of Maine in 1848. Deep-sea Captain George W. Kimball and his neighbors had started by felling tall trees; by November 1849 they had built their ship, the *California Packet,* and set sail. They arrived in San Francisco in September 1850 with 217 men, women, and children aboard. The group soon scattered; many went to the gold fields. An earlier settler from Maine, Rev. W.W. Smith, persuaded some of the families to come to the new town he was founding. Among the first homes built in the town was that of Captain Kimball, shown in the old drawing reproduced at right.

Chapter 4

Rev. William Wiggin Smith

Founder of Antioch Was a Preacher and a Carpenter

William Wiggin Smith and his brother, Joseph, were Campbellite preachers from Maine who first settled in New York of the Pacific (which later became Pittsburg) in July 1849, where William, a carpenter, constructed the first building -- an eating place and hotel. Shortly afterward the brothers pre-empted adjoining quarter sections and founded Smith's Landing, which became Antioch. The name was suggested by William at a basket picnic held at his home on July 4, 1851, attended by about 35 persons -- almost the entire population of the town.

51

Brick Schoolhouse Replaced Ship's Galley

The boys wore their hats at rakish angles and the girls dressed primly in white when they posed for this photograph around 1880. The two-story brick schoolhouse was built in 1869 at what is now Sixth and G streets. It was a more impressive building than the typical little red schoolhouse built by some other towns in that era. The $4,000 cost was raised by public subscription. Antioch's very first school had started at the same time the town was founded in 1851. Classes were held in a galley removed from an old ship. The teacher was twelve-year-old Adelia Kimball, daughter of Captain George W. Kimball. Writing about her experiences years later, Adelia said that the ship's galley "was small and dark, while out-of-doors was big and bright, and we had fine recesses." The brick schoolhouse shown above was replaced by a wooden Victorian-style building in 1890--which was razed in turn when John Muir School was completed in 1926.

When "F" Street Was a Railroad

A railroad on F Street? Don't say it cannot be, for here was Engine No. 1 headed south on Kimball (now F) Street, near the intersection of Adams (now Sixth) Street. The Empire Railroad started operations in 1878, hauling several hundred tons of coal to the dock each week from the Empire Mine in the foothills of Mount Diablo. This photo was taken in the 1890s. At that time the Congregational Church (built in 1891) had a steeple and the Beede family had a fenced corral. Bob Hale's house was behind the church and Doctor Wemple's house was a bit farther south. The top of the Will family's house can be seen in the background. The Waldie house was just below it. The church is still standing, but the steeple is long gone.

Turn of the Century:
The Rent-a-Horse Era

YOU RENTED a buggy, perhaps, from The Hunter Livery and Feed Stables, at the corner of Marsh and Boober (now Fourth and G) Streets, or you had them look after your horse. This picture was taken about 1900. At that time, Antioch had a population of 1200. Two steamboat lines landed boats at Antioch wharves every day, going to and coming from San Francisco. The first telephone company and electric company were just getting organized. The coal mines were going out of business, but the town had a bright future predicted for it as a manufacturing center.

The Remarkable
J. Rio Baker

Josiah Rio Baker was a dashing figure, often seen driving around downtown Antioch in the speedy little one-horse-power buggy shown at right, in an 1880 photo. With him (left) is a friend, Frank George, who was Mr. Baker's partner in a drug store on Wyatt (now Second) Street. J. Rio Baker was a member of the volunteer fire department, longtime secretary of the Masonic lodge, a partner in a hardware store (shown below), and a notary public. He later served as postmaster of Antioch and still later was elected county treasurer.

The Brown & Baker
Hardware Store

In 1890 the Brown & Baker Hardware Store occupied the northeast corner of Wyatt and Boober (now Second and G) Streets. In addition to the merchandise you'd expect, such as nails, farm implements, tools, etc., the store also sold furniture, carpets, wallpaper, stove oil, and other items for home and farm use. A sign over the main entrance advertised Eureka Stoves and Ranges, which were among the first mass-produced kitchen appliances. In this picture the people in front of the store are (left to right) Uncle Billy Forman, Ina Baker, George Hawxhurst, Jean Baker Turner, Josiah Rio Baker (in a cutaway coat and stylish straw hat), Ben Turner, and Frank Bigelow. The store changed its name and ownership over the years, successively becoming Antioch Hardware & Furniture Company, Trembath & Fredrickson, and Howse Hardware—and then it changed completely and became Famous Fashions, the place where a generation of Antioch's best-dressed women bought their clothes. Now, more than a century after the inception of Brown & Baker, there is a computer store on that corner.

John Donlon on Truck. Jay & John Belshaw Frank Wills Ed Rapp Will Purchase

Coal Miners Became Storekeepers, Started Antioch Cash Store

With a couple of delivery wagons out in front and the proprietors and employees posing for the photographer, here is the Antioch Cash Store as it appeared around 1890. John Donlon is the man sitting at the reins. Some of the others are Jay and John Belshaw, Frank Wills, Ed Rapp, and Will Purchase. The store sold work clothes, food stuffs, and a variety of general merchandise. It was started in the mid-1880s by Mortimer, John T., and Jay P. Belshaw. The Belshaws had been involved in the Empire Coal Mine and Railroad, which closed down in the 1890s. Charles M. Belshaw, son of Mortimer, became a state senator. His home at the corner of Seventh and E Streets was a showplace, built around a Queen Anne style tower. Considerably remodeled, it later become the home of Joe Baldocchi.

Second Street - Muddy in Winter, Dusty in Summer

BEFORE 1907, whoever had to travel on Wyatt (now Second) Street did not find the way paved for him. (That year saw the start of city paving.) All the streets were mud holes in winter and dustbins in summer. Antioch had its share of automobiles, as indicated by the parade heading toward the camera. On the left is the First National Bank, Stockton City Laundry, Home Bakery, Palace of Sweets, and Palace Drug Co. On the right is Delta Electric Co., Bank of Antioch, Kinnear Drugs, and the landmark Arlington Hotel. Did you notice the 5c beer sign?

The Arlington Hotel, A Favorite Stop For Travelers

The three-story Arlington Hotel, Antioch, known as "the traveling man's home," was a favorite stop for riverboat passengers and crews. It was built in the 1880s. It had 40 rooms, an elegant dining room, and a bar. The picture shows the hotel in 1902, with a number of local people out in front. The gentleman second from the left, standing, was George K. Beede, who ran the hotel for a while. However, most of the time the Arlington was owned and managed by Fred Dahnken, a German immigrant, whose hospitality and 24-hour bar were well known up and down the Delta. Mr. Dahnken also owned the Palace--a large rooming house in Antioch, and a saloon at the Santa Fe depot. He was the father of one of the partners in the gigantic T & D theater chain, which started in Antioch. Sitting in chairs on the front porch of the hotel are H.F. Beebe, Dave McCartney, Gabe Meyer, J.P. Abbott, and John Rouse. Looking down from the balcony are Josie Beede, young Sidney Beede, and Mrs. George Beede. The carryall -- pulled by two elegant white horses, with a Mr. Boothby (no one remembers his first name) at the reins -- picked up passengers from the riverboat docks and from the two train stations and brought them to the hotel, which was located on Wyatt (now Second) Street, between G and H Streets, right in the middle of the bustling downtown business district. The Bank of Antioch and Kinnear Drugs were in the same block as the hotel. Across the street were the Palace of Sweets and the Home Bakery, both fondly remembered by old timers for the treats they got as children. The hotel building was torn down in 1939 when the federal government bought the property as a post office site. A post office was never built at that location and the government later sold the property, which became a parking lot. This photo came from the collection of Dan McKellips.

Early Industries in Antioch

Antioch Lumber Company (left) was started in 1864 in the days when lumber came by sailing ship to the wharves. H.F. Beede bought into the business in 1882. It has been an Antioch institution for 111 years since then, operated by several generations of the Beede family.

The earliest manufacturers in Antioch included Albion Pottery, started in 1865; a soda works, a distillery, and three brick yards. In 1889 M.D. Keeney & Sons established a paper mill, which is shown at right. Following several mergers it became Fibreboard Paper Products. It changed names and owners since.

Other pioneer industries in Antioch were Western California Canners, Hickmott Canning Company, and Fulton Shipyard. Later arrivals were Crown Zellerbach Corporation, Kaiser Gypsum, and DuPont.

The Old Antioch Bridge: 53 Years of Service

In the years after the first World War the automobile came into its own. A demand arose for highway access to the islands of the Delta and for a route from Antioch to Sacramento. An auto ferry had been started by C.A. Lauritzen, a former riverboat captain, but it never became popular, mainly because the north landing, on Sherman Island, was 12 miles away from the nearest road. Drivers had to take their Model Ts over farmers' fields. In 1921 a campaign was started by Roy V. Davis, president of the Antioch Chamber of Commerce, to get a bridge built from Antioch to Sherman Island. Aven J. Hanford and Oscar H. Klatt of the American Toll Bridge Company decided to take on the project. They formed the Delta Bridge Corporation, hired Frank H. Reynolds to design the bridge, and got started building it in 1924. It was finished in 1926 at a total cost of $1.4 million. With completion of the bridge it was possible to drive from Sacramento to Oakland on paved highways. The bridge had a lift span in the middle to provide clearance for ocean-going vessels, with most riverboats traveling under the fixed span. It was privately owned until 1940, when the state bought it. In 1979 it was replaced by the new Senator John A. Nejedly Bridge.

Restaurant Was Built on Old Wharf

Frank Battaglin started operating the Commercial Hotel, at Second and I Streets, Antioch, in 1917. Later he ran the Red Front bar and the Santa Fe Club. And then he got his best idea: a restaurant on the old wharf at the foot of H Street. Previously, for many years, asparagus from the Delta had been unloaded from river steamers onto this wharf for transhipment via Santa Fe. The restaurant was built in 1948 and called the Riverview Lodge. Frank's son, Leo, was a partner from the start; another son, Larry, came into the business in 1954. The Riverview burned down in 1961 and was rebuilt. It has now been in business for 45 years. Larry's daughter and granddaughter are the third and fourth generations of the Battaglin family working at the restaurant.

The Great Snake of Antioch

You've heard fish stories and big foot stories and UFO stories. What makes the story of the great Antioch snake unique is that a whole town believed it.

For four months in 1934 the nation's newspapers headlined news items about a gigantic 30-foot python on the loose near Antioch. The whole affair started when Anthony Romano said he saw a monstrous serpent at the old coal mines south of town. Soon others claimed they saw it too, and a curator from the zoo in San Francisco mounted a safari. He found nothing, but the snake stories continued. Car drivers and their passengers reported seeing the huge reptile—now nicknamed "Aimie-Minnie"— wriggling along the sides of roads on the outskirts of Antioch.

The town was almost in panic; children were kept off the streets, and the fire department had an "early snake warning system" (four blasts of the fire whistle). A Hollywood film crew came to Antioch hopefully to photograph the great snake for a newsreel.

Then, on November 14, 1934, the *Oakland Post-Enquirer* ran a big headline on the front page, "Big Snake Caught at Antioch." According to the newspaper story, the huge python was captured in an abandoned coal mine near Somersville. Tear gas was poured into the shaft and the emerging snake was wrestled into a steel cage by several men and then hauled away to the ranch of E.F. Blowers, near San Francisco. The snake was reported to be 30 feet long and 6 to 8 inches thick.

And then it was announced, in the *Antioch Ledger,* that the snake would be exhibited at the American Legion Hall in Antioch. Hundreds of people paid 50 cents each (which was donated to charity) to see the great snake, which turned out to be a fake, made of old inner tubes carefully painted to resemble a real reptile.

The perpetrators of this hoax had started the snake scare by arranging nighttime sightings along lonesome roads. A motorist who was in on the secret would drive an innocent passenger or two past a prearranged spot where a car without lights would be pulling the snake (with a long rope) in the opposite direction. Years later Victor Parachini, one of the pranksters, said, "It was the most realistic thing. When I saw it operating it made my blood run cold."

Archie Roberts, now in his late 80s, is the man who made the rubber monster in his garage (there had earlier been a cloth snake stuffed with sawdust). His younger brother Verne (who served as mayor of Antioch in the 1960s) furnished us with this classic photo of Aimie-Minnie and her prankster friends. The man holding the snake's head was a Mr. Johnson (whose first name is unremembered). The others (left to right) are Vic Parachini, Archie Roberts, Dean Marvin, Al Flaherty, Mac McKinney, and Jim Quinn.

In a 1986 interview with a reporter from the *Oakland Tribune,* Mr. Parachini spoke about the snake scare: "I was 35 years old then. It was the depths of the Depression. We were just beginning to get over the really troubled period, and we had all this pent-up steam and enthusiasm and nothing to do. I wish I was 35 again."

Western California Canners Operated Throughout the Delta

ONE OF THE LARGEST enterprises in the Delta area was Western California Canners, which operated a cannery in Antioch, a warehouse in Pittsburg, and huge farms in the Byron area and on Bouldin Island. The company was started in 1933 by Vince and Bert Davi in Walnut Creek. In 1934 the Davi brothers moved to a waterfront site in Antioch. In the mid 1930s a subsidiary was formed — Western Farms — which grew asparagus, tomatoes, and other vegetables and grains on some 10,000 acres. A $1 million warehouse for canned goods was opened in Pittsburg in 1960. By that time the cannery in Antioch was packing 3 million cases a year, mostly tomato products and asparagus, labeled with many prominent brands, including Western's own Rialto brand. This aerial photo shows the canning plant and offices on the Antioch waterfront. Inside the buildings in the foreground tomatoes and asparagus went through a flume system for washing and then down conveyor belts for inspection, processing, cooking, and canning. In 1966 the firm was acquired by Ogden Foods.

Chapter 5

The Discovery of Coal Started a $20 Million Industry

Coal, the "black diamond" in the Mount Diablo foothills, was to build—and destroy—five towns, spur the growth of three others, and in 42 years of mining operations yield a $20 million harvest. It was discovered at Horse Haven Valley, six miles south of Antioch, by William C. Israel in cleaning out a spring on his land in 1855. Four years later, 3 1/2 miles west, Francis Somers and James T. Cruikshank discovered a larger vein, which was developed by the Black Diamond Mining Company and, in 1895, gave a new name—Black Diamond— to New York Landing (later called Pittsburg). The engraving reproduced above shows the Black Diamond mine during a typical working day, with a coal train coming in from the waterfront for another load from the mine bunkers. The buildings shown include offices, barracks, and warehouses. This mine and others accerlerated the growth of Antioch, Black Diamond, and Clayton and created the coal mining towns of Somersville, Nortonville, Stewartsville, Judsonville, and West Hartley. With the end of coal mining operations in 1902 Antioch, Black Diamond, and Clayton continued onward in new directions, but the coal mining towns disappeared. Wood from the buildings in those towns was used to build homes in Antioch and Pittsburg.

Coal Train at Somersville

Starting in 1866 the Pittsburg Railroad hauled coal for the Pittsburg Coal Mining Company to Pittsburg Landing (later the site of Dow Chemical), which was just east of New York Landing. (New York Landing was the original site of the town which later became Pittsburg.) This 1896 photo shows rail cars being loaded at a Somersville mine bunker. The coal was fed through large chutes to each car in turn as the train inched forward.

Stewartsville Mine Bunker

The photo below shows a Stewartsville mine bunker in 1882 with a group of visitors, dressed in their Sunday-best, posing in the foreground. Stewartsville was southeast of Somersville. Coal from Stewartsville's Central mine shaft was carried to Antioch via the Empire Railroad, as was coal from mines near Judsonville and West Hartley.

A School for Miners' Children Started in 1866

The first school in Nortonville was started by D.S. Woodruff in 1866. This picture, taken a few years later, shows the student body and Mr. Woodruff in front of the school building. The school was supported by a one per cent tax on miners' wages.

Most of the children came from the mining towns, but children from New York Landing also attended this school until 1874, when New York Landing got its own school. In its era the Nortonville School was one of the largest in the county.

Downtown Nortonville

Noah Norton built a house near the Black Diamond mine in 1861 and thus founded Nortonville, which became the largest of the coal mining towns--and one of the largest towns in the county, with a population of 1400. The photo at left shows Main Street, Nortonville, about 1870, with some of the miners and merchants lounging in front of the buildings. Even at its peak the town was primitive and raw looking. From left to right are the butcher shop, barbershop, a boarding house, a lodging house and Knights of Pythias Hall, and several other building.

Village Choir In Front of Granny Norton's

Most of the coal miners were from Wales. They brought much of their traditions and culture from the old country, including a love of music. Many were excellent singers. This is the Village Choir on Church Hill, posing for their picture on the grounds of the Nortonville Congregational Church. The choir was one of several groups that participated in community celebrations, the most notable of which was the *Eisteddfod,* an ancient Welsh festival which included competitions in singing, recitations, and compositions in prose and poetry. The house in the background of the photo belonged to Sarah Norton, widow of Noah Norton. She was the midwife of the town, affectionately called Granny Norton. (She became a legend after she died, with many persons claiming to have seen her ghost in the area.)

The End Of the Mines

Towns Were Deserted, Miners Moved To Washington

In the 1880s labor trouble and the steadily rising costs of production began to hurt the coal mines. Near the turn of the century water seepage and dwindling coal deposits forced the closure of some mines. In addition, better quality coal had been discovered in the state of Washington. The last feeble mining operation ceased in 1902, but before that a sailing ship had already carried most of the miners and their families to the new town of Black Diamond, Washington, to start anew. Three attempts to revive coal mining in the Nortonville-Somersville area in the 1920s and '30s proved futile and the idea was abandoned. Sand mining had started in the area and continued for some years, but eventually the sand mines were abandoned also. The mining area has become a regional park and the former mines may be visited by the public. Some homes in Pittsburg and Antioch were built of lumber salvaged from the mining towns and many residents of Contra Costa are descendants of the early miners.

Miners' Burial Ground on Rose Hill— "The Memory of the Righteous Is Blessed"

Lonely, windswept Rose Hill Cemetary was started in 1849 on the hill it is named for, between Nortonville and Somersville. A total of 92 gravestones were placed there, marking the resting places of Welsh and Cornish miners and members of their families, along with other Contra Costa pioneers. One of the best known personages interred there was James Kirker, frontiersman and rancher. Kirker Pass Road is named for him. A mysterious band of mounted Indians attended graveside services for Kirker, sitting in dignity on their horses a short distance from the burial site. When the ceremony was over the Indians silently rode away. History does not record who they were or where they came from. The cemetary has several tombstones with epitaphs written in Cymraeg, the ancient language of Wales. The epitaph of Elizabeth Jones comes from The Bible: "Coffawdwriaeth y cfrawn sydd fendegedig." The translation is: "The memory of the righteous is blessed." (Proverbs 10:7)

66

Chapter 6

The Beginnings of Lafayette

Elam Brown

Frontiersman and farmer Elam Brown had led a wagon train of settlers from the Midwest to California in 1846. In 1847 he purchased the Acalanes Rancho and 300 head of cattle for $900, which had traveled across the plains hidden in his wife's eight-day clock. The Brown family moved to the rancho in February 1848. Their first home was a frame house in the area now known as Happy Valley. Mr. Brown sold parts of the land to his two sons-in-law, Thomas W. Bradley and Nathaniel Jones. (The latter was first sheriff of the county.) Thus started the settlement that became the village and later the city of Lafayette. A lithograph depict-ing Elam Brown's farm in 1879 is reproduced above. The two-story family home can be seen at left. A pair of wagons, loaded with sacks of flour, drawn by six horses, is shown coming from the grist mill Mr. Brown had established nearby. At the time this picture was drawn Lafayette had a school, church, hotel, blacksmith shop, post office, and two taverns. Mr. Brown had served his fellow citizens as a delegate to California's Constitutional Convention in 1849 and as Alcalde of the Contra Costa District. He was later elected to two terms as an assemblyman, and then went back to his first love, farming.

Blacksmith 'Shot Off' Anvil to Celebrate End of Civil War

PETER THOMSON was Lafayette's blacksmith for 50 years. He's the man with the Uncle Sam beard, shown with an employee in the photograph, taken around the turn of the century. The blacksmith shop had been built about 1853 by Jack Elston, in a stand of walnut and locust trees. It was on the north side of Lafayette Plaza. Thomson went to work for Elston in August 1859, and bought the shop four years later. Thomson did a brisk business with townspeople, farmers, and travelers. He shod horses, repaired farm machinery and wagons, and made and fixed tools.

His work at the forge was vital to daily life in frontier times. The anvil shown in the picture is now on display at the Lafayette Library. It has an interesting story. When Thomson learned that the Civil War had ended, in April 1865, he celebrated by loading a hollow place in the anvil with powder, igniting it with a long red-hot poker—thus "shooting it off." The explosion cracked the anvil. He repaired it and shot off the anvil every Fourth of July from then on, but with not quite so much powder. After Thomson died in 1914, his son carried on the business until 1924.

Schools Came First For Early Settlers in Lamorinda

SCHOOLS WERE IMPORTANT to early settlers in the Lamorinda area. The first school in Lafayette was built in the 1850s on what is now Golden Gate Way, between First and Second Streets. Benjamin Shreve was the town's first teacher. The school was replaced in 1871 by the second school, on Moraga Road. The third school was somewhat larger, with a belfry and several classrooms. It was built in 1893 in front of the second school. The picture shows both school buildings in 1899, with pupils and teachers posing out in front. The teacher in the doorway, to the right, is Margaret Jennie Bickerstaff. The third school later became part of the Methodist Church on the same site. The belfry secton was dedicated for its historic interest May 6, 1973. The second school building was moved to Mount Diablo Boulevard in 1927. Other early schools in the Lamorinda area and the dates they were started are as follows: Willow Spring School, in what is now Moraga, 1855; Moraga School, on Moraga Way in Orinda, 1861; Mount Pleasant School, in Sather Canyon, 1863; Orinda Park School, 1882, and the Canyon School, 1917, still in use.

Miss Bickerstaff Taught School in Orinda, Lafayette, and Walnut Creek

Twenty-year-old Margaret Jennie Bickerstaff began her teaching career on September 1, 1892, at the Moraga School (later called Glorietta School), on Moraga Way near Glorietta Boulevard, in what is now Orinda. Right around that same time she posed for this photograph on her horse Topsy, which she rode to school every day for years. Her home in Lafayette was three miles from the school, going cross-country through pastures, dismounting to open gates in fences. In bad weather she took the road, which made the trip two miles longer. Notice her riding habit. Victorian equestriennes wore hats, gloves, and long skirts -- and rode sidesaddle to protect them from the immodesty of straddling the horse. Those were the days when legs were unmentionable; they were called "limbs," but not in mixed company. The dirt lane in the picture later became Mount Diablo Boulevard. Miss Bickerstaff had 34 pupils in her classroom, from first grade through the ninth. She was paid $60 a month. In ensuing years she taught school in Lafayette, Pacheco, Walnut Creek, and Saranap. The place where her home stood on Mount Diablo Boulevard in Lafayette is now the site of Diablo Foods, a supermarket started in 1968 by Edwin Stokes and Sal Vallelunga. The redwood trees planted by Miss Bickerstaff still stand in the store's parking lot. Miss Bickerstaff retired after a long career, revered as one of the pioneers of Contra Costa.

Old Tavern Became Historic Landmark

THE WAY SIDE INN was a hotel and tavern on the stagecoach road between Oakland and Walnut Creek. It was built in 1894 by Edward J. Brady & Company near the old site of the grist mill built by Elam Brown, founder of Lafayette. It faced on Lafayette Plaza. T.H. Reed, a later proprietor, gave it the name Way Side Inn. This picture was taken about 1910, when automobiles were replacing horse-drawn vehicles. The sporty touring car parked in front of the inn was a 1909 Reo. As you can see from a sign partially hidden by a tree, the inn had just changed hands, with a Mr. Schlenker as the new proprietor. The business suffered some setbacks during the next decade and the building was abandoned. It was purchased in 1922 by Gerhardt "Pat" Medau and his wife, Lizzie.

They fixed up the building and converted it into a meat market, using the old hotel rooms as their living quarters. In 1925 the Medaus' daughter, Lorelda, opened an ice cream parlor in the building after the meat market moved to Mount Diablo Boulevard. In succeeding years the old Way Side Inn building housed a number of businesses, including the Quality Bakery-Fountain, Guinevere Thompson's Dress Shop, Etta Roger's Beauty Salon, several barbershops, a temporary Greyhound Bus Depot, and—from 1950 through the early '70s—Jack Hageman's insurance office. Karen Wilcox's Wayside Antiques next occupied the building for five years, and then, in 1978 it became the Way Side Inn Thrift Shop. It was dedicated as a place of historical interest on June 13, 1970.

The Pioneer Store Provided Groceries, Work Clothes, and News

THE PIONEER STORE was the center of community life in Lafayette for many years. Originally Benjamin Shreve's general store, it was established in 1855. The first Lafayette post office was started in the store in 1857. The store moved into a new building on the plaza in the early 1860s. In 1902 it was acquired by Robert E. McNeil, who renamed it the Pioneer Store and ran it until 1935. It was the place where townspeople exchanged news and gossip, and—in the early 1900s—where they talked on the telephone, the only one in town. Some afternoons people would listen to music on the grammaphone in the store or play horseshoes or baseball out in front. McNeil loved to wrestle and would go outside to take on any challenger. This picture was taken about 1928. The people,

from left to right, are Robert E. McNeil; his wife, Gertrude; her first cousin and namesake, Gertrude "Trude" Russi; the McNeils' grandson, William L. McNeil; the Russis' daughter, Dorothy, and the McNeils' daughter, Alice. The Pioneer Store carried groceries, drugs, dry goods, men's work clothes and shoes, farm equipment, hardware, stove oil, gasoline, and coal. The bins along the corner at left contained dried fruits, macaroni, beans, etc. The store was sold to George Hinckley in 1935, then to Mr. and Mrs. Vincent Lombardo in 1941. The Lombardos moved the store to a new building at First and Golden Gate Way in 1945, keeping the name, Pioneer Store. The old building facing the plaza became, in later years, a bicycle and toy shop called the Handlebar.

Lafayette Post Office In 1904

THE FIRST post office in Lafayette was started in 1854. It was called Acelanus (a variation of the spelling of Acalanes), with hotel owner Milo Hough as the postmaster. When Hough moved his hotel to Walnut Creek in 1855, this post office was discontinued. Then Benjamin Shreve, owner of a general store, applied for a post office for the community, first requesting the name "Centerville." Since that name was already in use elsewhere in California, the name "LaFayette" was used as a second choice. It was later spelled with a small "f." The post office was established in Shreve's store, where it stayed for 30 years. After Shreve's death, William Boardman became postmaster, succeeded by Carrie Hough Van Meter in 1904, not too long before this picture was taken. Mrs. Van Meter served for 23 years in this building, which was located at the northwest side of the intersection of Mount Diablo Boulevard and Moraga Road. The girl is Pearl Van Meter, the postmaster's daughter, on her horse, Pegasus. The home of the Van Meters is to the left. The family's cat also posed for this picture (lower left).

The Lafayette Improvement Club was organized in 1911 at a meeting in the Pioneer Store. In February 1912 the group voted to build a town hall. A lot on Moraga Road and $200 were donated by Frank and Rosa Ghiglione. More money was raised by holding a series of dances in local barns. Then a stock corporation was formed, with local citizens buying shares for $1 each. The town hall was built by contractor Albert Gerow. It opened officially on May 1, 1914, with a bean feed downstairs and a dance upstairs. On the following night a grand ball was held. This photo was taken just three days later (May 5th) on Sybil Wilkinson's birthday. That's her new red buggy parked out in front, a birthday present. The two young men are friends of hers from Oakland. The Lafayette Town Hall has served for nine decades. It has been used by PTAs, athletic clubs, churches, schools, the American Legion, Lafayette Forum, garden clubs, Boy Scouts, Camp Fire Girls, etc. It has been used for meetings, dances, suppers, classes, and as a nursery school, library, and recreational center for children. During World War II part of it was a barracks for Navy Pre-Flight cadets from Saint Mary's. It was used for numerous theatrical presentations by the Lafayette Playshop and the Straw Hat Revue in the 1940s and '50s. Since 1958 it has been the home of The Dramateurs, a group that was founded in 1944 in Orinda. The town hall was dedicated as a place of historic interest on October 14, 1978.

Lafayette Town Hall Served Many Purposes

How Do You Spell Reliez?

If you've ever driven on Reliez Station Road and wondered what Reliez station is or was, here's a picture of it, taken Sunday, July 20, 1919, as a train rolled by. Only, in those days they spelled it "Raliez," as you can see by the sign. This was one of the smallest depots on the Oakland, Antioch & Eastern line (later called Sacramento Northern). We have the names of two of the boys standing in front of the 8- by 10-foot station: 14-year old Harry Williamson (left) and his 12-year-old brother, Melvin (third from left). As noted on previous pages, this suburban railway served many communities in the county, some of which no longer have train or bus service. A few of the station names would be unfamiliar to Contra Costans now: Las Juntas, Saranap, Burton, Pinehurst, Madrone, Havens, as well as Raliez—or Reliez—which is now part of Lafayette. The railway cars were powered by trolley wires.

The Days of Nickel Ice Cream Cones

PAT'S ICE CREAM - SODA was the name of the fountain that Lizzie and Gerhardt ("Pat") Medau opened for their daughter Lorelda (also nicknamed "Pat") in 1925. It was located in the historic building facing the Lafayette Plaza that had been a tavern and hotel called the Way Side Inn in the early 1900s. The Medaus bought the old building in 1922 and operated a meat market there. After the meat market was moved around the corner to Diablo Street, they opened the fountain. Lizzie Medau (who insisted that her name was Lizzie, not Elizabeth) is shown behind the counter. One of the best customers was her grandson, Rothery McKeegan, in front of the counter. Nickel ice cream cones and penny candy were best sellers. One penny bought as many as 10 pieces of candy in those days. The price list on the wall shows some more bargains: Sodas . . .15¢, Root Beer . . . 10¢, and so on. Root beer was drawn by a spigot from the barrel at right. The cylinder on the counter was a straw dispenser. Cigars from Havana were popular with drummers (traveling salesmen), who stopped by to ask directions and have a cup of coffee for the road. When the fountain closed it was succeeded by a number of different businesses, which took their turns at occupying the building—including a bakery, dress shop, beauty parlor, several barbershops, bus station, insurance office, antique shop, and—finally—the Way Side Inn Thrift Shop. The little boy in the picture grew up to be an Air Force colonel.

Firehouse Became A Summer Home

Here is the Lafayette Fire Department about 1930, with four fire engines and three volunteer firefighters out in front. This firehouse was in the center of town at 984 Moraga Road. It was scheduled to be replaced in 1949, so Mickey Meyers bought it, dismantled it, and moved it to Clear Lake, where it was reassembled to become a summer home for the Meyers family. Meyer's neighbors in Clear Lake were amused that the front of the house still read "Lafayette Fire Dist." A new firehouse was built on the site of the old one on Moraga Road. This latter building also became obsolete and it became a nursery school.

Reservoir Was Finished Four Years Late

Planned as part of a project to bring mountain water to the East Bay, the Lafayette Reservoir was started in 1927, but not finished until 1933, about four years behind schedule. The delay was caused by an unexpected settling of the massive dam in September 1928, which caused huge cracks. Work was stopped for three years while engineers and geologists watched for addtional movement. In 1932, after it was determined that the shifting had stopped back in 1928, the dam was redesigned to be quite a bit wider than the original plan (for safety's sake) and construction resumed. The aerial photo shows the completed dam at left center. The tall tower near the dam is part of the pumping system, where water is piped into and out of the reservoir. The old highway (now called Mount Diablo Boulevard) is shown in the mid-foreground, winding its way by several farms. The reservoir stores drinking water for parts of Alameda and Contra Costa Counties. It has become a recreation area, operated by the East Bay Municipal Utilities District, open to the public all year for fishing, boating, picnicking, and hiking—but no swimming is allowed. The first trout were planted in the reservoir in the summer of 1969 and many thousands have been planted every year since. In addition to trout the reservoir contains bluegill, black bass, black crappie, and several types of catfish.

Lafayette Horse Show Of 1936

VISITORS AND ENTRANTS from all over California attended the Second Annual Lafayette Horse Show, Saturday and Sunday, August 29 and 30, 1936. It was held at Dr. O.D. Hamlin's ranch, near the intersection of Saint Mary's Road and Solana Drive. The horse show was held in conjunction with the town-wide Fiesta de '49 (named for the '49ers of Gold Rush days), which featured dancing each evening at Lafayette Town Hall, a bathing beauty revue, boxing and wrestling matches, and a parade on both Saturday and Sunday mornings, with 300 horses and a dozen floats. The annual fiesta had been started in 1934, with Dr. Daisy A. Hetherington as general chairman. The horse show was added the following year at the instigation of tavern owner Lou Borghesani, with Charles Shuey as general manager and Dr. Hamlin as president of Lafayette Horsemen's Association, sponsors of the show. Months of planning and hard work went into each year's horse show, which brought fame to the small town of Lafayette during the late 1930s and early '40s. A huge arena was leveled and fenced, with a grandstand built along one side (at left in the photo). Parking was provided for several hundred trucks and cars. Some of the events listed in the program included pleasure horses, saddle stallions, pintos, buckskins, hackamores, stock horses, and colts in hand.

Tunnel Road Was the Main Drag

Here is downtown Lafayette in 1941—a strip of businesses on Tunnel Road (which later was renamed Mount Diablo Boulevard). In the foreground at the extreme right is Garrett & Garrett real estate and insurance office and a barber shop. The building was errected a few years before by Colonel Manuel Garrett, a World War I veteran and Lafayette civic leader. It was designed by architect Carr Jones of Orinda, who had worked with Bernard Maybeck, and it was supposed to be a prototype for future Lafayette commercial edifices, an idea which was before its time and unfortunately not followed. The building was remodeled in 1987 and won an architectural award. It is now occupied by the elegant Tourelle Café & Bar. Colonel Garrett had offered to errect a similar building for the post office, but with typical bureaucratic thick-headedness, the W.P.A. turned him down and built the uninspired white box you see next door. The postmaster was Emelia S. Schutt—and whatever the deficiencies of the building, she got the mail delivered on time, an achievement many postmasters could emulate today. Next down from the post office is the Lafayette Pharmacy, which also had a fountain and Bear Photo Service. Next is Gibson Hardware, where you could buy Boysen paints, an extensive selection of pipe fittings, and 'most any kind of tool. Next is Johnnie's Roundup, a cowboy-style bar which had started in 1935. Some of the customers would tie up their horses in back. Now known simply as The Roundup, it is still in business and has essentially the same phone number (Lafayette 4817 in 1941; 284-4817 now). Next is Mickey Meyer's Groceteria, which shared a building with the Lafayette Meat Market. If you look close you'll see Lou's Lafayette Inn on down the road.

Straw Hat Revue Played to Full Houses

The Straw Hat Revue was a group of actors and singers from the University of California in Berkeley that performed every summer from 1945 through 1949 at the Lafayette Town Hall. They played to full houses with political satire and comedy sketches. The material they performed—both music and dialogue—was written by members of the group. The Straw Hat Revue got a lot of attention from the media, with rave notices in the San Francisco Chronicle and other papers. Performances attracted patrons from all over Northern California.

Chapter 7

Walnut Creek Started as Crossroads Stop

Location, location, location! The site of Walnut Creek just *had* to become a town. First called The Corners, it was at a spot where four Mexican land grants came together: San Ramon, Las Juntas, Cañada del Hambre, and Arroyo de las Nueces y Bolbones. It was also the main crossroads of Contra Costa, where the wagon trail from Martinez to San Jose met the trail from Oakland. These trails became the first highways in the county (later replaced by freeways) and are now called Main Street and Mount Diablo Boulevard. In 1849 William Slusher built a cabin at the crossroads, and then, in 1855, Milo J. Hough put up a hotel and store nearby, called Walnut Creek House. A year later Hough added a blacksmith shop. A number of settlers built homes in the area, a school was started in 1857, and another store was started in 1859. In 1860 the land was subdivided into lots. This was when Walnut Creek officially became a town. A post office was established also in 1860 and more

homes and stores were added during the next few years. Brown & Company started a stage coach line in 1864, with routes to Oakland and to San Ramon. The Methodist-Episcopal Church was dedicated in 1872. In 1880 William B. Rogers, a former San Ramon Valley farmer and retired San Francisco police officer, built the hotel shown above, which became known as "one of the best houses of entertainment on the Pacific Coast," according to an early historian. This photo, taken in 1890, shows the Wilson Brothers stage coach from Oakland about to leave for Danville. The photographer inveigled as many people as he could to pose for this picture; that way he could sell more prints. Did you notice the two men and a little girl standing on the porch roof? The Rogers Hotel later became Las Palmas Restaurant and Cocktail Lounge and stayed in business through the 1950s, when it was torn down to make way for a new fireproof structure at 1336 Main Street.

Walnut Creek Meat Market: A Century Of Service on Main Street

One of the busiest places on Main Street in the 1890s was the Walnut Creek Meat Market, owned by Arthur Williams. The building at left was a slaughter house. Three horse-drawn wagons were used to deliver meats and groceries to customers in Walnut Creek , Alamo, and the surrounding area. Charles Moisan is shown at the reins of the wagon at left. Frank Donner is the man standing in front of the store, and Mr. and Mrs. Williams are in front of the wagon at right center. A Mr. Peralta is on horseback in the background at right. The store was popular right from the start and business was brisk, with animals coming to be slaughtered each day, delivery wagons coming and going, and butchers working 10 or more hours a day in the shop, hanging carcasses and cutting meat. The market was purchased in 1910 by Joseph and Fred Lawrence (sons of the founder of the Danville Meat Market) and their brother-in-law Al Stephen. The store later moved next door to 1432 Main Street and the slaughter house was moved to a 50-acre site out of town. Members of the Lawrence family have continued to run the store. It moved to Alamo a short time ago.

Walnut Creek in 1910

Traffic was so light in 1910 that people could stop their cars in the middle of Main Street, and then get out and have a conversation, like the folks in the above photo. But the merchants were pretty busy for a small town with only a few hundred inhabitants. The stores served not only the residents and nearby farmers, but also travelers passing through.

In the photo you can see (from the left) A.G. Cameron's wagon & buggy shop; First National Bank; R.N. Burgess's real estate office and his competitor Putnam Realty next door; a garage, and a pool hall, among others. The building with twin towers also can be seen in a similar view of the street taken 30 years later (page 86). On the right side of the street Rogers Hotel is the only business fully visible.

Store employees and their families posed for the picture (right) of Valley Mercantile on the corner of China (later Cypress) Street and Main. The store sold clothing and shoes. Those poles standing up along the edge of the sidewalk aren't for parking meters; they're hitching posts for horses.

First Festival in Walnut Creek Celebrated Harvest; It Was the Forerunner of Walnut Festival

A Harvest Festival was held in Walnut Creek in September 1911. This was the first such celebration in the town. The photo shows Mary Ridgeway, queen of the festival. She later became Mary Lichens and served as city clerk. Runners-up in the queen contest were Gertrude Walker and Sybil Brown. The festival was held right in the middle of downtown. Main Street was decorated with huge piles of baled hay and grapevines for the occasion. There was a big street dance, with a lively orchestra on a wooden bandstand, and lemonade, beer, and food being sold at booths along the wooden sidewalk, and there was a big parade with marching bands, clowns, horseback riders, and floats from various towns in California. The festival was a forerunner of the city's annual Walnut Festival, which was started in 1938 at the instigation of John T. Schroder and other Walnut Creek businessmen.

The Walnut Creek Train Station Was a Busy Place in 1910

This 1910 photo is deceptively calm; the Walnut Creek train station was often the center of activity. There were mixed passenger-freight trains night and day, going to Livermore and other destinations on Southern Pacific's San Ramon Valley loop, with connections to main-line trains going everywhere. A surrey from the Rogers Hotel would be there to meet every train. Wagon-loads of cherries, pears, peaches, apricots, walnuts, and hay were arriving constantly for shipment to markets in Oakland, San Francisco, and many other places. Livestock was often shipped into or out of town too; there were cattle corrals just south of the station with feeding and watering troughs. Just before noon each day wooden crates of Langendorf bread came in from Oakland, to be sold for 5 cents a loaf. Behind the station was an old swimming hole, frequented by naked boys in the summer, and there was a hobo jungle nearby, where campfires burned nightly. Clerks at a nearby store had orders never to turn a hobo away when he asked for a handout. The clerks sacked up portions of coffee and bread in advance for the "Weary Willies." The station had been built in 1891, one of several along the loop in Contra Costa county. Passenger service was never profitable on this line and was suspended in 1912, but the depot continued in use for freight into the 1960s, when competition from truckers finally closed it. The defunct station was then jacked up and moved on rollers a few hundred yards south of its original location, restored and slightly remodeled, to become a restaurant.

Walnuts arrive for processing.

Walnut Growers plant.

Walnut Growers Shipped Thousands
Of Tons from Walnut Creek

Neil "Jack" Harrison,
Manager of Walnut
Growers Association
1920 to 1943

Native black walnut trees grew profusely in the valleys and along the creeks in central Contra Costa. Early farmers realized that walnuts could become a cash crop. After wheat farms lost their profitability in the 1890s, mile after mile of walnut orchards appeared in the area, developing rapidly after World War I. In 1920 the local farmers organized the Contra Costa County Walnut Growers Association. The first officers were Frank Bancroft, president; Ed Smith, vice-president, and A.C. Gehringer, secretary-treasurer. Neil Harrison was appointed manager and a plant was built in Walnut Creek to process and pack the nuts for shipment. The plant processed 250 tons the first year. Production increased year by year as more members came into the association. The plant was expanded in 1923, 1924, and 1926. In 1937 a second plant was added and another in 1951. By 1958

there were more than 900 grower-members in Contra Costa, Alameda, Merced, and Stanislaus Counties. The packaging operations were moved to a plant in Stockton, built by the state walnut growers association, with which the local association was affiliated.(The state organization had changed its name to Diamond Walnut Growers in 1946.) The Walnut Creek plant was kept for grading, sizing, and bleaching. In 1958 the local plant was shipping 7,000 tons per year. This has all changed. The walnut orchards in Contra Costa have given way to tracts of ranch-style homes. The original walnut growers plant was converted to an art gallery and theater. A few years ago the building was replaced by a palace, also used as an art gallery and theatre, one of many new buildings in a farmers' town which has become a city of stockbrockers and corporation managers.

Big Fire in 1921 Scared City Council into Organizing a New Volunteer Fire Department

A big grass fire broke out on July 4, 1921, that threatened the destruction of downtown Walnut Creek. Fireman Guy Spencer went out to fight the blaze with a single helper, according to a diary he kept. He soon realized that the fire, which started in the hills above Mount Diablo Boulevard would be too big for his small crew to fight. He called to Oakland and Berkeley for reinforcements, which arrived in two hours, and the fire was stopped just short of downtown. The close call scared the city council into organizing a new volunteer fire department. An additional fire truck was purchased and able-bodied adults and high school students were placed on the volunteer list. By the time this photo was taken in 1944 Walnut Creek had this firehouse on Bonanza Street, seven vehicles, and three full-time employees: Chief Guy Spencer, Captain William Nottingham, and Captain Frank Graham.

Remembering El Rey

If you're a Walnut Creek oldtimer you may have thought nostalgically about this corner. You are looking south on Main Street on an early fall day in 1938. El Rey Theatre was where you went to see the latest Hopalong Cassidy episode at the Saturday matinee. This was the new theatre, opened in 1936. Your parents went on Tuesday nights for free dishes. The older Ramona Theatre, just down the street. showed mostly "B" pictures after El Rey opened.

Chick's Eats was where you got the best hamburgers in town. In back of the little diner was a deck above the creek (which had not yet been cemented over) with tables and chairs for *al fresco* dining.

El Rey Market, operated by H.C. Cherrington (who served for a time as mayor) later became a drug store. Just down the street from the theatre was Lawrence Chrysler-Plymouth, with a gas pump out in front. The showroom was only big enough for one car; the other new cars were parked in the alley next door. Pillsbury's Stationery started on this block in 1953 and is still there.

The left corner, which included a Union Oil station, became the site of a new city hall. The right corner became the site of the prententious glass-and-brick Civic Plaza Building, with a sculpture in front that looks like a huge pizza, minus two slices, standing on its edge.

In 1940 Main Street Was Also the Highway

You can see most of the stores there were in Walnut Creek in this 1940 photo of Main Street, looking north from the corner of Mount Diablo Boulevard on a Saturday afternoon. The big map on the wall of Arthur's Liquors was helpful to thousands of travelers; these two streets were also the main highways through town; freeways hadn't been invented yet. There was a Standard Oil Station on the corner next to Arthur's (the gas pumps aren't visible in this photo) and a lot of drivers used the map to figure out where they were going, while the attendant filled their tanks. (Self-service gas stations hadn't been invented yet either.) The liquor store was operated by Chester Arthur for 38 years. The businesses on the left side of the street, from foreground to background, include , after Arthur's, the Army-Navy Surplus Store, Walnut Beauty Shop, and several other stores--and

then we come to Bradley's Pharmacy and Fountain, in the building with towers in front. Some old timers remember the machine in Bradley's front window which made a round ice cream bar on a stick called a chocolate-coated moon. It cost a nickel, about half of a kid's daily allowance, but it was worth it. Mr. Bradley served a while as mayor and lived to be 100 years old. Looking down the right side of the street you can see the Shell garage, Bank of America, Western Auto, El Curtola Hotel, a jewelry store, another drug store and several other stores. At Curtola's corner there was a bridge across the creek leading to the Southern Pacific depot. One of the oldest businesses on the street, but not readily visible in the photo, was Mauzy's Plumbing, which has been run by four successive generations of the same family.

Dollar Ranch Hosted Fashionable Parties, Later Became Rossmoor

Sketch by Sylvia Rhoades

R. Stanley Dollar, Senior, a former executive of his father's Dollar Steamship Lines, purchased the Joseph Napthaly ranch in Tice Valley in 1930. He and his son, R. Stanley Dollar, Junior, developed the ranch into a 2,200-acre estate, where they raised horses and Hereford cattle. The senior Dollar had a house with an ivy-covered clock tower, shown in the sketch at left. His son had a similar house nearby. Many parties, attended by rich and famous people, were held on the ranch during the three decades of the Dollars' residency. In 1956 there was a barbecue party on the ranch for delegates to the Republican National Covention (which was being held in San Francisco) with President Dwight D. Eisenhower as the guest of honor. Suburban developments crowded in on the ranch in the late 1950s and the Dollar family decided to sell. In 1960 negotiations began between the family and Ross Cortese, which in 1963 resulted in a proposal for a senior community which was approved by the City of Walnut Creek. Thus began Rossmoor (originally called Rossmoor Leisure World, with a trademark wrought iron representation of the earth twirling out front). The homes of the Dollars have become clubhouses, now surrounded by residences and a golf course, but where mule deer still graze, seemingly unbothered by golfers or cars.

Lommel's Creamery Was Also the Greyhound Station

Richard A. "Dick" Lommel was raised on a farm. He learned how to make ice cream from his father, Otto, who was an instructor at the University of California at Davis, where he taught ice cream, butter, and cheese making. Otto Lommel was a graduate of the Swiss Agricultural School.

In 1939 Otto Lommel and two sons, Dick and Arle, purchased property on Main Street to build the creamery shown in the picture at right. In the 1940s the family opened additional creameries in Calistoga, Bella Vista (West Pittsburg), and Antioch, with Dick running the Walnut Creek operation.

In 1944 this also became the Greyhound Bus agency, with dozens of diesel buses arriving and departing daily, transporting hundreds of commuters and other travelers. Every weekday morning and evening the creamery was enveloped in a cloud of smelly diesel exhaust fumes. In the first year of operation the Walnut Creek Lommel's had sold 1,000 gallons of ice cream per month; by 1957 it was selling 5,000 gallons per month. Dick Lommel was usually there, greeting his customers by name. This writer remembers working for the city's weekly newspaper, the *Walnut Kernel*, in the late 1950s and having coffee breaks at Lommel's. This place, with its huge plaster ice cream cone on the roof, was a meeting place for merchants and shoppers —and a landmark for many years.

There Was Heavy Traffic on Main Street Back in 1953, Too

Heavy traffic is nothing new in Walnut Creek, and here is a 1953 picture of Main Street to prove it. You're looking toward the intersection with Mount Diablo Boulevard, with gas stations on facing corners.

Arthur's Liquors was still a familiar landmark, and continued to be for another generation.

There was a wide variety of traditional stores you'd expect to find on any Main Street in any town: jewelers, shoe stores, butchers, grocers, druggists, hardware stores, haberdasheries, cafes, etc.

Broadway Shopping Center (background) had just started in 1951 on land purchased from the pioneer Botelho family—the first regional center in Contra Costa—with Penney's and Sears-Roebuck facing each other across Broadway Plaza. Auto buffs will recognize cars in this photo that have since become collectors' items, including vintage Hudsons, LaSalles, and Cadillacs.

Mount Diablo Boulevard was still part of the highway to Oakland and Main Street was still part of the highway to Martinez in that pre-freeway era.

Post-War Trend:

The Drive-In

After World War II, with the end of gas rationing, people could drive their cars again. Drive-in movies and drive-in restaurants were springing up everywhere. They took a while getting to a little town like Walnut Creek, but finally—on January 10, 1957—Mel's Drive-In opened on North Main Street between Arroyo Way and Ygnacio Valley Road. Mayor Edward Counter took part in grand opening ceremonies.

The building was designed by an award-winning architect, Mario Gaidano of San Francisco. It had a brick exterior with burnt-orange porcelain interior walls; booths upholstered in white leather (the real thing, not plastic), and terrazzo floors.

Patrons could choose to dine either inside the dining room, or on the patio, or in their cars, waited on by car-hops. Teens loved to congregate at Mel's—and the place was also popular with young families, who could pile the kids into the back seat and go out to dinner without having to cope with highchairs or tots' table manners.

JOEL CLAYTON
Born in England, 1810. Migrated to United States when he was in his late 20s. In 1850 he led a wagon train across the continent.

Chapter 8

Clayton Was a Miners' Town

The town of Clayton was founded in 1857 by Joel Clayton to provide provisions and entertainment for local coal miners. The Clayton Hotel (above) was a tavern and lodging place, built by Romero Mauvais, a Frenchman, the same year the town started. It was destroyed several times by fire and rebuilt each time. Nearly everyone in town got into this picture, taken in 1875. The hotel continued in business over the years under a succession of owners. It became just a tavern, "Tat's Place," run by Tat Murchio (and later by his brother, George), in the 1930s and '40s. In 1946 the building was leased by Chubby Humble and became the Pioneer Inn, a popular restaurant. A fire in 1951 destroyed the second floor and the Pioneer Inn was rebuilt with one story, with a new redwood dining room added. The building still contains some original beams dating back to 1857. The Pioneer Inn was later operated by John Jawad for many years. It has since changed name and ownership.

The Trette Blacksmith Shop (right) was a landmark at Oak and Main Streets for eight decades. It was started in 1859 by Matthew F. "Doc" Nottingham. This picture, taken in the 1890s, shows (left to right) blacksmith Harry Trette, who bought the shop in 1880; his son, Rudolph "Dutch" Trette; Burt Curry, and J. Collins, who was a dancing teacher. Harry Trette ran the shop for 50 years. His son "Dutch" worked there from 1898 to 1942.

Charlie Rhine
Sold *Everything*

Charles Rhine, a Polish immigrant, formed a partnership with Joel Clayton in 1857 to start a general store in the new town of Clayton. First located in a remodeled house, the store was immediately successful. In 1863 Mr. Rhine was able to buy out his partner. In 1878 the business moved into the building shown at left. The people of the town were all dressed up for a special civic occasion. Three women were looking out of the upstairs windows behind signs which said, "E Pluribus Unum," the U.S. motto; "Eureka," ("I have found it!"); "Veni, Vidi, Vici," ("I came, I saw, I conquered")--all familiar to a first-year latin student, and one sign in English, "Welcome to Our Chief." Charlie Rhine sold just about anything his customers wanted: groceries, farm tools and machinery, clothing, fabrics, and sundries. Men's suits cost $7; shoes were $2.50 a pair. You could buy an oil lamp, a bottle of whiskey, or an insurance policy. A pair of eyeglasses sold for 75 cents. There were even gourmet items, such as oysters, lobsters, salmon, and fancy cheeses. Charles Rhine General **Merchandise Store** was the major business in Clayton for half a century.

A Fun-Loving Town

The people of Clayton have always celebrated life exuberantly. There were several saloons—gathering places for miners at first, then vineyardists and orchardists and townspeople. And, in the old days there were two social halls, where many dances and parties were held in the fun-loving town, most of them lasting all night, with dramatic performances, songs, skits, and an orchestra for dancing, and lots of food and drink. A ticket to one of these events is reproduced below.

Masquerade
Ball
RHINE'S HALL, CLAYTON
Friday Evening, Jan. 31st, 1896.
Gents, in costume, 50c; Ladies, in costume, free; Spectators, 25c.

Vineyards & Wineries Flourished in Clayton

From the 1860s on, vineyards and wineries spread out around Clayton, including those of Paul DeMartini, Glen Terry, and J. Levi, and the largest of them all—the Mount Diablo Vineyards and Winery. There were 500 acres of wine grapes in the area in 1902, according to the *Richmond Record*. Some of the wines from Clayton were winning top prizes at the California State Fair, and DeMartini's port and sherry won blue ribbons at the Louisiana Purchase Exposition at Saint Louis in 1903.

Clayton Had Two Stage Coach Lines

Stage coaches carried mail, bank deposits, and passengers between various towns in Contra Costa up until 1913. Jack Atchinson and his brother, George, took over operation of two of the stage lines in 1898. Jack drove the larger four-horse stage coach (built by D.G. Barnett of Pacheco) from Clayton via Concord to Martinez and back. George took the smaller two-horse stage on the run between Clayton and Antioch. They drove every day except Sunday, under government contract. The mail had to get through, regardless of weather conditions. Sometimes in the winter months George, wearing oilcloth clothes, had to ride horseback, leaving the coach and passengers behind, because the roads were too muddy to carry a vehicle. However, most of the year George was seated on the front seat of the small stage coach, as he is in the picture. The three passengers look like they are enjoying the ride. George left Clayton every morning at 7, went via Nortonville and Somersville to Antioch, arriving at 11 a.m. He did business errands, fed and rested the horses, and then started out again, going back through Somersville and Nortonville and adding Stewartsville to the itinerary, arriving in Clayton at 4 p.m. He was required by his contract to carry a .45 Colt gun when driving. However, he never faced a holdup and never had to use the gun. The horses were shod at Bott & Smith's blacksmith shop in Concord, four shoes for $1.

Early Car In Clayton

Hilda Rhine Atchinson posed in 1921 at the wheel of one of the first cars in Clayton. Incidentally, another Atchinson—Wil, grandson of Jack Atchinson—became a car dealer in Pleasant Hill.

Living in the Country

Oldtime Clayton Was a Haven for People Who Liked a Simpler, Less Hectic Lifestyle

CLAYTON GRAMMAR SCHOOL (above left) had some 50 pupils in 1913, when this picture was taken. Wilda Chapman was the teacher and a Mr. Graves was the principal. Every May Day was a holiday for the schoolchildren. Wagons loaded with families would travel to Mitchell Canyon for a big community picnic. The school was located on a hill above Mitchell Creek, on the same site as the Mount Diablo Elementary School which later replaced it.

THE CLAYTON CASH STORE (below left) on Main Street was the successor, in a way, to Charlie Rhine's old store, providing groceries, hardware, and dry goods to the 1,000-or-so inhabitants of the town. The post office was also located in the store.

THE OLD METHODIST CHURCH (below right) at Oak and Center Streets, circa 1903, later became a Christian Endeavor Hall, a headquarters for the Grange, and a community meeting hall. The Congregationalists and Presbyterians also built a church, of stone, on Center Street, which was unfortunately razed by a later purchaser of the property.

Marsh Creek Springs Park Hosted Two Million Visitors

If you lived anywhere in the Bay Area during the 1930s, '40s, and '50s you likely were among the two million visitors to Marsh Creek Springs Park during that period. On its 210 acres near Clayton there were three swimming pools, a riding stable, a dance pavilion, a small steam railroad, and various playgrounds, cabins, ballfields, and picnic spots. One of the pools is shown above, with a snack bar at left. The park was the creation of Gerould L. Gill, who bought 90 acres of land six miles east of Clayton around 1930. Mr. Gill personally supervised the construction of concrete-lined swimming pools and the other facilities of the park, working side-by-side with his employees. Land was added to the park from time to time, bringing its total size to 210 acres by 1940. Mr. Gill was a cousin of Weldon Bagner

Cooke, the pioneer aviator who was the first to fly over the Bay Area, piloting a plane built in Pittsburg. Both men were descended from the remarkable family which founded Lockeford in San Joaquin County. After being graduated from high school in Oakland Mr. Gill had mastered four trades: steel fabrication, shipbuilding, interior decoration, and construction work--all of which gave him the abilities necessary to create his park. After Mr. Gill's obvious success several other parks similar to his were started in the same area. Marsh Creek Springs and some of the other parks have continued operating, but are not as well attended as in previous years, probably because of the proliferation of free public parks and competition from other types of recreational facilities.

Chapter 9

Alamo Pioneer "Squire" Stone Lived in This House

SILAS STONE, 61, and his wife came to California from Iowa in 1853 in a wagon train. Their son, Albert, was captain of the wagon train. The Stones purchased land near Alamo in 1853 and built this house in 1855, from redwood lumber hauled from Canyon by ox teams and wagons. "Squire" Stone, as he was called, was Alcalde of the Alamo District and a member of the board of trustees of the Union Academy, an educational institution established in Alamo in 1860. This home, a handsome one for its day, was located at 2144 Stone Valley Road, and was occupied by three generations of the Stone family before it was torn down in 1954. The interior walls were planks covered by wallpaper. The windows were set between upright timbers, running from ceiling to floor. Interior plumbing of the nine-room house was limited to the kitchen sink. The inset shows Silas Stone and his wife in their later years.

Alamo School Girls Wore High-Button Shoes in 1897

HIGH-BUTTON SHOES, leg o' mutton sleeves, pinafores with lots of ruffles—this was what little girls wore to school in the Gay Nineties. Some of the boys wore neckties and Eton jackets. Many of the girls had corsages and some of the boys wore boutonnieres for this picture, which was taken at the Alamo School on April 15, 1897. The young lady holding the slate was Lilias Stone. She later became Mrs. Elmer Short. All of the girls wore long hair in those days—and none of the boys did. Getting to school meant buttoning shoes or boots with small implements called shoe hooks, brushing one's hair 100 strokes, and, often, riding one's horse to school. Leg o' mutton sleeves were puffed at the shoulders and tapered to the elbow or wrist. The first Alamo School was built on land acquired from Mary Ann Jones in 1876. She was the widow of Alamo's first postmaster. This building was destroyed by fire. It was rebuilt several times on the same site.

Delivering Meat And Eggs in Alamo

Good-looking young Joseph E. Lawrence posed with his team and delivery wagon in front of the Henry Hotel in Alamo around the turn of the century. The hotel had been built by the Howard Brothers in 1858 and named after the proprietor, Henry Hoffman. It was one of Alamo's landmarks until it was torn down in 1954 to make way for a gas station. Joe Lawrence and his brothers started their meat market in

Danville in 1897 and it operated there until 1941. They also acquired a store in Walnut Creek (see page 81) which has moved to Alamo and is still in business, run by Joe's grandson. The Danville market sold meat, poultry, milk, cream, and eggs, most of which were the products of local ranches. Note Joe's jaunty bow tie and fedora hat, which most young men wore in those days. The apron was the uniform of his trade.

Alamo Post Office Was Also a Grocery Store

THE ALAMO POST OFFICE was established in 1852, the first in the San Ramon Valley. John M. Jones was the first postmaster and the post office started in his adobe home, which was across the road from the site of the present day Alamo Plaza. The Alamo Post Office was then the only one between Martinez and Mission San Jose. Mail was delivered by horse and rider at first, and then by stagecoach. The post office moved many times over the years. It was once in the Henry Hotel, and another time in a small building where the parking lot of the Elegant Bib Restaurant was later located, and various other places, depending on the desires of whomever was postmaster. However, it stayed in one place for 26 years, from 1910 to 1936, in the two-story building shown in the photo, which was known as Bell's Post Office Store. There was no home delivery in those days, so farmers and townspeople had to come get their mail. While they were there, the proprietor figured, they could also pick up groceries, work clothes, cigars, candy and sundries. You are looking north on Route No. 21 (now called Danville Boulevard) at the intersection of North Avenue (now known as Las Trampas Road). The roads were unpaved—better suited to horses and wagons than to automobiles. One of the men on the porch may have been David Crockett Bell, who was postmaster from 1905 to 1923. Three of Bell's children later served as postmasters: Roy D. Bell, from 1923 to 1936; Harriet (Bell) Hunt, 1936 to 1944, and Bertha (Bell) Linhares, 1947 to 1960.

Early Pioneers Got Together in Danville

AMONG THE FOREMOST men of their time, the gentlemen pictured above came together to be honored at a picnic in Cox's Grove, Danville, in the late 1880s. Most of these men—and their families—had come to the San Ramon Valley in the 1850s, when it was a verdant wilderness. They built homes, planted crops and trees, raised farm animals, made roads and streets, dug drainage ditches, and started shops and stores. By the time this picture was taken, the towns of Alamo, Danville, and San Ramon were thriving, due in large part to the efforts of these pioneers. Some of the names are still familiar because their descendants still live in the valley—and because there are roads, streets, and places named after some of them. From left to right: Albert W. Glass, son of rancher and merchant, David Glass; John King; Milton Labaree, Danville rancher; William Meese, Sr., San Ramon rancher; Levi A. Maxcy, Tassajara rancher; Edward McCauley, owner of the Railroad Hotel, Danville; unidentified man; Samuel F. Ramage, east county rancher; Lee Parker; Edward Shuey, Walnut Creek merchant; Albert W. Stone, leader of westward-bound wagon train in 1853 and son of Silas Stone; Samuel Moore, Charles G. Goold, Danville banker; John P. Chrisman, Danville businessman; Myron W. Hall, pioneer walnut grower who first grafted English walnuts to black walnut roots; David Glass, San Ramon rancher who also started the first trading post in Alamo; unidentified man and child; William Z. Stone, rancher; Nathaniel Howard, rancher; Robert O. Baldwin, San Ramon rancher whose grandson, John F. Baldwin, became one of Contra Costa's most beloved congressmen; James O. Boone, Danville settler, descendant of the famed Daniel Boone; William Cox, who had a 200-acre farm between Danville and San Ramon; George McCamley, San Ramon cattleman, and Elisha Harlan, son of early pioneer Joel Harlan. These pioneers are long gone, but their contributions to the development of Contra Costa County will long be remembered.

Halverson Family Specialized in Transportation

DANVILLE LIVERY STABLE was the place where one could rent a horse and buggy, like the one in the center of the picture, for $1.50 a day—or a surrey, with two horses, for $3 a day. It was owned and operated by John E. Halverson, a Norwegian immigrant, who had been a sailor on a lumber schooner for 20 years and had then married and settled down in Tassajara Valley in the 1870s to raise horses. The family moved to a new home on Hartz Avenue in Danville in 1891. Halverson built the livery stable the same year on a large park-like lot which fronted on School Street, with access on the sides to Front Street and Hartz Avenue. The Halverson family planted many redwood trees on the property. The stable was popular with townfolk, who kept their horses and vehicles there.

Halverson's customers included traveling salesmen, who arrived on the train and then rented buckboards to carry huge trunks of merchandise about the countryside. Hayward milk dealers rented wagons, like the one at left in the photo, to haul milk and cream to their customers. Large wagons from the Danville Livery Stable carried hay and grain from the valley to docks at Pacheco to be loaded on barges. Roy Halverson, John's son, got into the business as a teenager at the turn of the century. He specialized in operating the rigs to Hayward and Pacheco. The Danville Livery Stable, like many other once-familiar institutions, has passed from the scene, but members of the Halverson family are still active in various enterprises in the San Ramon Valley.

Downtown Danville At Century's Turn

HERE IS Front Street in Danville as it looked in the early 1900s. It was the main street then (and until the 1920s, when Hartz Avenue took over). From left to right: Cohen's Store, Tiger Alley (now Prospect Aveue), Gibbons Harness Shop, Joe McCeil Barber Shop, Conway Store, Post Office (with the Danville Library upstairs), Blacksmith Shop, and Close's Store (with the I.O.O.F. Hall upstairs). It must have been a busy day in Danville, judging from the number of horses and wagons. Did you notice the early automobile? It's just to the right of the barberpole.

Look Out! Here Comes the Alligator!

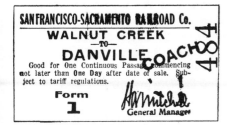

A ticket used on the Valley's electric line.

IN 1914 an old baggage car was turned into a hybrid trolley car, which commenced a run between Saranap (now part of Walnut Creek) and Diablo, traveling down Hartz Avenue in Danville on the way, as shown in the photo. The car—half coach and half baggage and freight—took commuters to Saranap every weekday morning, where they transferred to Oakland-bound trains. Those commuting to San Francisco took a ferry from Oakland. The trolley also met the transportation needs of those wishing to travel from one part of the county to another, to shop or to visit friends. The line was called the San Francisco-Sacramento Railroad and was a subsidiary of the Oakland, Antioch and Eastern, which became the Sacramento Northern. The trolley was noisy and subject to frequent breakdowns. Passengers had to open their umbrellas inside the car when it rained. There was a pot-bellied stove to keep the car warm on cold days. The Valley people delighted in the eccentricities of their electric trolley car and dubbed it the Alligator or the Toonerville Trolley, after a comic strip of that era. Losing passengers to the automobile in the 1920s, the Alligator made its last run on March 1, 1924. In less than a month the tracks were torn up and the little railroad became a memory.

Danville Panorama, 1914

This photo shows most of Danville in 1914. The Southern Pacific depot is in the center of the picture. Note the two railroad cars in front of the depot. Just to the left, partly hidden by trees, is the spire of the Presbyterian church. The large buildings closest to the camera are the Wiester and Flournoy warehouses. The Hartz Ranch is in the foreground. Danville had a population of less than 400 in 1914. It was a country town, where farmers could buy supplies and socialize. The Grange was probably the most important organization. The products of the countryside included walnuts, pears, and prunes in the valley-- and grain and hay in the hilly areas. This produce was shipped by rail and trucks to destinations all over the West.

Shopping in Danville in the 1920s

If you lived in Danville in the 1920s a shopping excursion might have included the Danville Emporium, shown at left, with the proprietors, Belle and Joseph Foster, standing in the doorway. It was located on Hartz Avenue, at the site later occupied by J & F Office Supplies. The Emporium welcomed browsers, who stopped to chat with the good-natured Fosters. The store advertised that it sold "Dry Goods, Millinery, Notions, Etc.," which included such items as clothing, bolts of cloth, needles, thread, ribbons, dolls, greeting cards, knick knacks, and gifts. The store got its first telephone listing in 1923; the number was 42J. This was changed in 1925 to 29J. Some of the other stores you might have encountered while shopping during that era would include A. Binse's Danville Home Bakery, Danville Shoe Store (run by M.J. Medina), and McDonald's Drug Store, where you could have bought Miller's Quality cream, Haas fresh candy, and Brunswick phonographs and records. You might also have dropped into the Danville Shaving Parlor, Al Hanis's Barber Shop, Williamson's Confectionary, and Acrees Grocery Store.

U.S. Postage Stamp
honored O'Neill.

America's Greatest Playwright Lived in This Danville Home

America's greatest playwright, Eugene O'Neill, and his wife, Carlotta, lived in this home in Las Trampas Hills above Danville from 1936 to 1943. Mr. O'Neill used part of his Nobel Prize money, awarded in 1936, to build the home at the upper end of Kuss Road. The O'Neills named their home Tao House, which comes from a Chinese word that can be translated "right way of life." It is pronounced "dow."

Working in a study with a spectacular view of Mount Diablo, the playwright wrote some of his best known works here, including *The Iceman Cometh, Long Day's Journey into Night, Hughie,* and his final play, *Moon for the Misbegotten,* which won four Tony awards in 1974. Mr. O'Neill's failing health forced the couple to move to a San Francisco hotel in 1944, where medical treatments were more readily available. Mr. O'Neill was pictured on a U.S. postage stamp issued in 1967 (shown at left, above).

Tao House was placed in the National Register of Historic Places in 1971 and was designated a National Historic Site in 1976. Under the jurisdiction of the National Park Service it is open to the public. However, Kuss Road is private and the people residing there have an inordinate aversion to strangers. The home can be reached only by a special tour bus at very limited times. For further information one should call (510) 838-0249. The sketch of the home was made by this writer in 1976. The two-story section in the middle was added after Mr. O'Neill left and has since been removed.

Speedy Trotting Horses Were Bred At Stock Farm

THE OAKWOOD PARK Stock Farm was one of the leading horse and cattle breeding farms in the nation from the late 1870s to 1912. It covered 6000 acres, including what is now the Diablo Country Club, the town of Diablo, and the southern slopes of Mount Diablo, almost to the summit. Some of the employees of the stock farm posed for this picture about 1895 in front of the farm's elegant carriage house. The man in the surrey at right may well have been the owner, John Boyd. The Oakwood Park Stock Farm had its own race track and many buildings in the Swiss architectural style, including the carriage house, a huge horse-training barn, the owner's home, a dairy house, a laundry, a billiard hall, and numerous corrals and pens. There was a reservoir in the hills which delivered pure mountain water to all parts of the stock farm through some 40 miles of pipe. The trotting horses raised at the stock farm broke many racing records and the farm's Shorthorn and Devon cattle were sold as breeding stock in the U.S., Hawaii, South America, and Japan.

" . . . and the Winner is . . . *Oakwood!*"

HARNESS RACING was a passion among Contra Costa pioneers around the turn of the century. There were race tracks in Concord, Walnut Creek, and Oakwood Park Stock Farm, to list a few. Some of the fastest trotting horses in the world were raised at the latter place. One of those horses, named "Oakwood," is shown above, winning the big Decoration Day race in Pleasanton on May 30, 1912. The time around the one-mile track was 2 minutes and 16 seconds. (This was the track, then privately owned, which later in 1912 became part of the Alameda County Fair Grounds.) The owner of "Oakwood" was a Danville blacksmith, A.J. Abrott, who proudly took home a big loving cup, the major award of the day, and received congratulations from his friends. It had been a very hot day in Pleasanton—well over 100 degrees Farenheit—so the time wasn't up to some of the records set by other horses from the stock farm. The celebrated stallion "W. Wood" came to the front at the age of four years with a record time of 2.07. Also "Agatata" made a record of 2.09 at three years of age and "Diablo" went over the one-mile track at the stock farm at 2.09¼ at four years of age. The days of the stock farm were ending, however. Robert N. Burgess bought it in late 1912 and began converting it into a country club—the beginnings of the present day community of Diablo.

Diablo Country Club Started in 1912

THE DIABLO COUNTRY CLUB and the town of Diablo were born in 1912, when Robert N. Burgess bought the Oakwood Park Stock Farm. He converted the farm into a country club, with residential lots adjoining it. The former billiard hall of the farm was remodeled into a clubhouse and the old residence became the club's Inn, where members and their guests could stay. The picture shows the interior of the clubhouse about 1916. Note the Victorian wicker chairs and oriental rug. This room has not changed much since then, but the main bar was installed in the area shown at right. The building was renovated in 1948, with a huge ballroom added. In 1916 Mr. Burgess started a separate company, the Mount Diablo Villa Homes, to handle the sale of lots. Several substantial homes were built that year for William Letts Oliver, Edwin Ball, George C. Browne, and Mr. Burgess himself. Also in 1916 the Blackhawk Ranch was founded on 1250 acres purchased from Burgess by Ansel Mills Easton, who built a fine residence and started raising Shire horses and Shorthorn cattle.

Famed Cattle and Horses Were Bred at Blackhawk

WORLD FAMOUS for its purebred Shorthorn cattle and prize Shire horses, the Black-hawk Ranch comprised 1,250 acres in the southeastern foothills of Mount Diablo. The ranch was started by a Hillsborough millionaire, Ansel Mills Easton, who bought the land from Diablo Country Club developer Robert N. Burgess in 1916. It had been part of the fabulous 6,000-acre Oakwood Park Stock Farm. Easton took his son-in-law, William A. Ward, into partnership with him. Easton & Ward spared no expense or effort to create an outstanding ranch. The aerial photograph shows some of the ranch buildings and corrals in 1920, with the foothills in the background. The proprietors and their families lived in a beautiful 15-room mansion (not shown above) which had been designed by famed architect Louis Christian Mullgardt. It is still standing. In 1934 the ranch was sold to Raymond C. Force, retired president of the Caterpillar Tractor Company, who brought Here-ford cattle and Arabian horses to Blackhawk. In 1956 the ranch was bought by Castle & Cook Ltd. and Helemano Company Ltd. of Honolulu. The ranch was sold again in 1964 to G. Howard Peterson of Peterson Tractor, who remodeled the large home. In the mid-1970s Mr. Peterson sold most of the ranch to Blackhawk Devel-opment Company, which has subdivided the property for ostentatious homes for highly paid sports figures, business kingpins, and other rich folks.

The First Frame House in San Ramon Valley

LEO NORRIS left Missouri and crossed the plains in a wagon train in 1846, looking for a new life in California. After traveling about the state for several years, he and a partner, William Lynch (who had come around the Horn from New York), settled on the 10,000-acre San Ramon Rancho belonging to Jose Maria Amador. Norris bought a square league from Amador, which amounted to 4,450.94 acres. In September 1850 Norris and Lynch built the first frame house in the San Ramon Valley. (Before that time there had been several adobes and a small redwood shack on the property.) The Norris family and Lynch moved into their new home two weeks before Christmas in 1850. The two-story house was remodeled and added to during the ensuing years. Eventually it had 13 rooms. On the first floor there were two bedrooms, a parlor, dining room, kitchen, wash room, store-room, and walk-in clothes closet. Upstairs there were five bedrooms and a bath-room. The house is pictured above as it looked about 1900, when it was half a century old. At that time it was the home of William Norris, Leo's son. The lady in the buggy was William's wife, Margaret, then in her late 60s. This was the back of the house. The front was a little fancier, with shutters on the windows, a wide porch, and a picket fence. The house continued in use till 1950, when it burned down, 100 years after it was built. William Lynch, who was 23 years younger than Leo Norris, had married Leo's daughter, Mary, in 1853, and bought some land from his father-in-law, which became part of Lynchville, later called San Ramon.

Small Rural Schools
In the Southern Valleys

There were small rural schoolhouses all over Contra Costa from the earliest times of settlement. Here are three that served the San Ramon Valley and the nearby Sycamore and Tassajara Valleys.

The San Ramon School was built by Elbridge Dole, a carpenter, in 1867. There were two rooms, with 13-foot-high ceilings. Albert J. Young was the first teacher. The building was in use for 83 years--until 1950, when a new three-room school was built nearby, on Crow Canyon Road.

The Tassajara School stood in a grove of shade trees. It had a delightful little cupola on top, "carpenter gothic" decorations on the porch, and a flagpole in front. It is thought to have been built about 1888.

The Sycamore School, according to the first teacher, Mary Hall, "was organized in March and on April 23, 1866, provided with a set of Wilson's School and Family Charts with the Manual and Sheldon's Book on Object Lessons, the school began. A blackboard was supplied on June 4th . . ." First classes were held in a small shanty until the building shown in the photo was completed on September 15, 1866. Mrs. Hall's register recorded 17 pupils. Charlotte Wood, daughter of a pioneer family, attended this school and then, when she grew up, taught there from 1890 to 1921. She was honored in her later years by having a new school named after her.

SAN RAMON SCHOOL

TASSAJARA SCHOOL

SYCAMORE SCHOOL

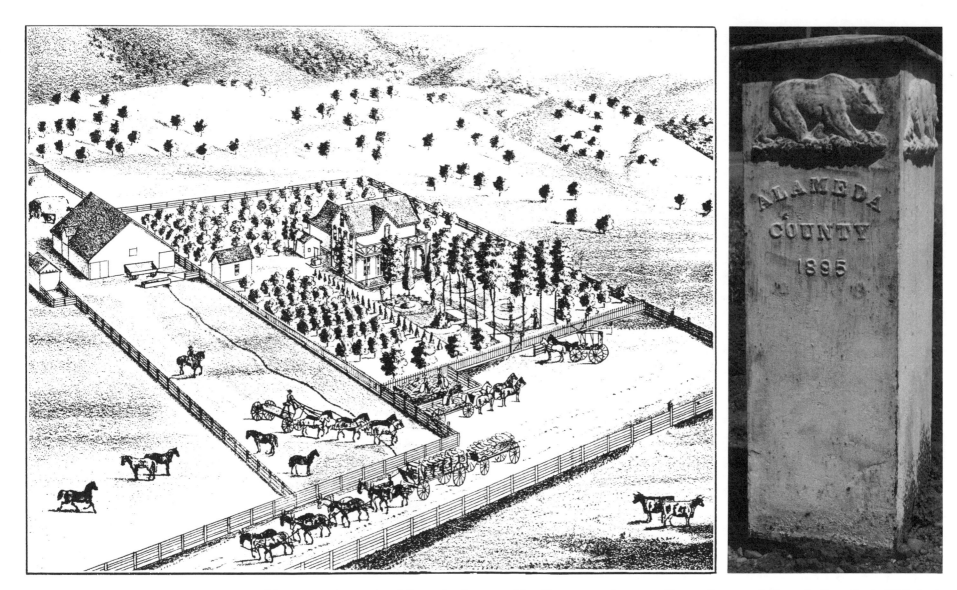

San Ramon Pioneer Had His House On County Line

JOEL HARLAN was one of the early pioneers of San Ramon. He came to California from Indiana in 1846 in a wagon train with his parents, grandmother, brothers and sisters, in-laws, and nieces and nephews. As a young man of 18 Joel made his own way in California, going into partnership with his cousin, Jacob Harlan, in a number of enterprises, including shingle splitting in Canyon, a riding stable and a dairy in San Francisco, and gold prospecting on the American River. Joel bought land from Leo Norris in Amador Valley in 1852 and built a house near the present site of Dublin. When the state legislature set the boundary between Contra Costa and Alameda Counties in 1853, Joel Harlan's house was picked as a landmark which the boundary went through. He tore this house down in 1857, using the materials to build another near the village of San Ramon. Shown in the lithograph above, it was a two-story home, surrounded by shade and fruit trees. The boundary marker, shown at right, was originally installed at the site of Harlan's first house, but was later moved to the corner of San Ramon Valley Boulevard and Amador Boulevard, Dublin. A descendant of Joel Harlan, Harlan Geldermann, was one of the founders of Diablo Bank.

The Sounds of Hammer and Anvil

THE CLATTER of horses' hooves and the sounds of hammer and anvil filled the air in early San Ramon. The placid rhythms of rural America sang out reassuringly. Olsson's Horse Shoeing and General Blacksmithing shop was located on Old Crow Canyon Road in San Ramon. The shop was started in the late 1880s by Andrew Olsson, a Swedish immigrant. Olsson and his employees shod horses, repaired agricultural machinery, and made tools for the farmers and townsfolk of the San Ramon Valley. The photo shows the shop about 1910. Standing in front (left to right) are Edwin Olsson, the proprietor's youngest son; his brother, Reuben; an unknown man; Andrew Olsson himself; Oscar Olsson, the oldest son; Fred Wiedemann, a local farmer, and Mark McIvor, a businessman. The two wagon drivers on the right are not identified. The firm sold Studebaker wagons and buggies, advertised by a sign on the building. The Olsson family home is shown in the background. The shop was later owned by M. William Fry, who continued in business into the 1920s. The Olsson family has played an important part in the history of Contra Costa County right up to the present. Oscar Olsson opened an electric store, garage, Nash auto dealership, and a service station in Danville; became a constable; served as a county supervisor from 1924 to 1932, and then became superintendent of the county hospital. Andrew Olsson's other sons enjoyed long careers in banking and industry and his daughters became teachers. Oscar's son, James R. Olsson, long served as county clerk.

Just a Few Stores Provided Goods and Services in San Ramon

Up until the 1950s the population in and around San Ramon consisted of about 50 or 60 farming families. The two business firms shown here, plus a couple of blacksmith shops and another small store, provided most of the community's needs.

The town had been a busy overnight stopping place for travelers in the 1870s, with several small hotels and Chinese laundries.

From the 1880s onward, H.C. Hurst's General Merchandise store offered groceries, hardware, farm tools, ladies' and gentlemen's finery, and other items. The store was a communications center where neighboring farmers could meet to exchange news and opinions. Also, the store served as the post office. Henry C. Hurst was postmaster from 1884 to 1915 and his son, Harry, was postmaster from 1915 to 1924.

In 1887 Wells Fargo opened an express office in the

store, which aided farmers in getting crops rushed to important markets. The store was also the office of Pacific Telephone. Not overlooking any possible need for services, Harry Hurst was an agent for a Hayward firm of undertakers.

The 1911 photograph (above) shows the elder Hurst standing in front of his establishment.

On August 11, 1924, William C. Fereira bought the big old general store, including all of the stock in trade, the fixtures, the furniture in the upstairs living quarters, and the building itself for a total of $2,750. He and his family moved in and continued the business for four more decades. Mr. Fereira also became the postmaster, in 1929, and kept that job for 34 years.

With the growing popularity of auto travel Mr. Fereira found it profitable to put a couple of gasoline pumps out in front in 1926—sort of a forerunner to the convenience stores of today.

The Thorup Shoe Shop, just a hundred feet or so away from the general store, was not just a shoe repair shop like the ones you see today. Peter A. Thorup (shown standing in the photo) and his helper made shoes to order for hundreds of loyal customers. The lasts you see shelved on the wall were wooden models of customers' feet. When a customer ordered a new pair of shoes it would be made on the last—and would usually fit perfectly.

Peter Thorup also repaired shoes, of course, and he also repaired saddles and harnesses—vital services in a farming community.

Mr. Thorup had another business, too, in later years. He put up a small hotel/roadhouse behind his house on Thorup Lane, which was frequented by local people and travelers.

The general store and the shoe shop are both long gone. San Ramon has grown a lot, and it's still a great town; but one can't help feeling a bit of nostalgia for old times.

The Men Who Ran the Ranch

THOMAS B. BISHOP

JAMES H. BISHOP

Bartlett Pears Made San Ramon Famous

THE LABEL reproduced above was affixed to boxes of extra fancy Bartlett pears shipped all over the world. The sweet firm fruit from the Bishop ranch added to the fame of San Ramon Valley as a fruit-producing region. Thomas Benton Bishop, a San Francisco corporation attorney, had bought 3,000 acres of the Norris League of the old San Ramon Rancho in 1895. This property became the famous Bishop Ranch. It was 1½ miles square, between Norris Canyon on the west and the Southern Pacific Railway on the east. The first enterprise of the ranch was raising some 400 head of beef cattle. Frank Rutherford, hired as superintendent in 1904, expanded the ranch's operations. A walnut orchard was planted in 1909. The pear orchard, covering 300 acres, was planted in 1911. During the next decade pure-bred Shropshire sheep started grazing on the land,

and peaches, prunes, grapes, and tomatoes were added to the list of crops. As the ranch expanded its productivity it became an important source of employment to many workers. The ranch headquarters had a superintendent's house, offices, machine shops, dehydrator building, foreman's house, commisary, tool sheds, and bunkhouse. There were additional farm buildings and dwellings on other parts of the property, plus a large warehouse and shipping shed on the spur of the S.P. tracks, which formed the eastern boundary. When Thomas B. Bishop died in 1906, one of his four sons, James H. Bishop, took over as president of the company. The ranch was sold in 1950 to Robert Crown. It changed hands several times in the 1970s. In 1978 Sunset Development Company purchased a 585-acre parcel which is being developed as Bishop Ranch Business Park.

Pacheco Was Once the Largest Town in the County

The village of Pacheco was laid out in 1857 on land purchased by William Hale, H.H. Fassett, and Dr. J.H. Carothers at the head of navigation of Pacheco Slough, four miles from Suisun Bay. At that time the slough was deep enough for ocean-going sailing vessels; Pacheco became one of several shipping points for wheat and other produce grown in Contra Costa. In October 1866 the *Contra Costa Gazette* reported that more than 600,000 sacks of wheat had been delivered that month to warehouses in Pacheco to be loaded on outgoing ships. The next month the newspaper noted that the streets of Pacheco were so crowded with wagon teams carrying wheat to the harbor that crossing the streets was impossible. Because of its importance as a port Pacheco became the largest town in the county. Main Street was lined with stores on both sides. The Solme Bros. Pacheco Cash Store, shown below left, sold groceries, farm implements, and work clothes. Another notable building was Elijah Hook's two-story Farmers' Block, built in 1860. The lower floor housed a general store and a Wells Fargo office; the upper floor was occupied by the *Contra Costa Gazette*, which was published in Pacheco from 1861 to 1873. The principal landmark in Pacheco was a steam-powered flour mill, four stories high, shown in the sketch below right. It was built in 1857 by William T. Hendrick on land he bought from George P. Loucks, one of the early settlers. At this time Pacheco also had a lumber yard, soda works, leather shop, brickyard, saddle shop, blacksmith shop and two hotels. Pacheco did not fare well: the flour mill burned down in 1867; an earthquake wrecked the town in 1868, and then a succession of fires and floods hit during the next few years. Pacheco Slough filled with silt and was no longer navigable. By 1870 most merchants and residents had moved to the new town of Concord or to other places. The flour mill did get rebuilt and continued in operation till 1912, under a succession of owners, but the rest of the town was virtually deserted. Pacheco continued as a quaint country village until the 1960s, when the population explosion brought tract homes and SunValley Shopping Center. Two Pacheco people deserve a special place in history: Annie Loucks, teacher at Pacheco Grammar School, beloved by several generations of former students, and Dr. Mariana Bertola, physician, humanitarian, and president of a unique California organization, Native Daughters of the Golden West. Two forerunners of modern agricultural machinery were developed in Pacheco: the Standish Steam Plow and the Dalton Gang Plow.

Chapter 10

This picture of Pacheco Roller Flour Mills was drawn by a traveling lithographer in 1895.

Pacheco Floods and Fires Helped Bring About the Founding of Concord

As we mentioned on the previous page, the town of Pacheco had been hit with numerous disasters in the 1860s: an earthquake, several fires and floods, and its main *raison d'etre*, Pacheco Slough, filled with silt and therefore ruined for navigation. Three men, who can truly be described as nice guys, came along and donated land to the beleaguered Pacheco peo-

ple in a new town a few miles to the east. The three men were Salvio Pacheco, his son Fernando, and his son-in-law Francisco Galindo. The town they started was originally called *Todos Santos (All Saints)*, and was nicknamed *Drunken Indian* by some irreverent American settlers, but soon after was renamed *Concord*, a name which stuck. Among the first of the Pacheco refugees to take advantage of the offer

of free land, in June 1869, was Samuel Bacon, whose store is the first one on the left in this early photograph. About the same time Charles S. Lohse put a machine shop across the street from Bacon's store, while John Brawand and George Gavin built themselves homes in the new town. The photograph shows, in addition to Bacon's store, most of the businesses on Salvio Street, looking east from the intersection of Galindo Street, not too many years after the town was started. There were several general stores, a hotel, and many saloons on this street. If you look closely you can see about two dozen people, including children, in this picture, standing on the wooden sidewalks and dirt street. They had waited patiently while the photographer made all his adjustments and then

finally recorded their images on a glass negative—to be saved for posterity. In addition to the buildings shown here there were two blacksmith shops in the town, one just behind the photographer on the other side of Galindo Street and the other two blocks away to the east and a block south. Historic preservation was not thought of in Concord's early years. Neither of the blacksmith shops and not a one of the buildings in this picture still stands.

Concord Had Two Blacksmith Shops

When Concord was founded in 1868 it was a tiny farm town, surrounded by wheat fields and cattle ranches. There were more horses and cows than people. Two blacksmith shops soon started and were kept busy, making and repairing agricultural implements, painting carriages, and shoeing horses. With forge, anvil, and hammer they made all sorts of tools, wrought iron fences, and other items. One of the shops was Boyd and Jaquith's, pictured at right, located at the north side of the intersection of Salvio Street, Galindo Street, and the road to Pacheco (now called Concord Avenue). Concord's original Presbyterian Church was nearby. One of the partners, Joseph Boyd, became the first mayor of Concord when it was incorporated with a population of 700 in 1905. The other blacksmith shop, Beute & Bauman's, had been established in 1872 at the northeast corner of Grant Street and Willow Pass Road, facing the plaza. In 1884 Henry Bott and Thomas Smith took over that shop. Below is a picture of their shop, with the partners standing in the doorway along with Mr. Bott's children. The Bott family lived in the little house at left. The shop thrived. The partners built a bigger building on the same site in the late 1890s. Years later the corner became a livery stable and still later a gas station. In 1975 a new building was constructed on the site for a title company. In 1980 it became a savings and loan office.

One of Concord's Founders Built This House

The Galindo family had been California colonists for two generations when Francisco Galindo married Salvio Pacheco's daughter, Manuela, and came to live on the great Rancho Monte del Diablo about 1850. This is the house that Don Francisco built--as it appeared in the 1880s, surrounded by fields and orchards, with the Chinese cook house at left. The two-story frame building was something of a departure from the adobe ranch houses built by a previous generation of Spanish settlers. Many descendants of Don Francisco have lived in this grand old house. The City of Concord has closed in around it, but it still stands on Amador Avenue. The house is durable enough and important enough historically that it is not likely to share the fate of historical buildings which have been torn down in the past by unthinking bureaucrats, but one hopes that it will continue to be used as a residence and not turned into a Disneyland-style museum.

The Concord Hook and Ladder Company

It Was the Town's Leading Organization, Both for Its Vital Function and as a Social Group

The Concord Hook and Ladder Company was organized in April 1879. It was the town's most important organization, both for its vital function and as a social group. Dances, suppers, and socials were held to raise funds for equipment. In 1883 the company built a firehouse on Mount Diablo Street, across from the Concord Plaza, now called Todos Santos Plaza.

The group photo of the volunteer firemen was taken in the 1880s in front of the firehouse. *Top row (left to right):* Henry Ivey, Philip Klein, Dr. H.G. Thomas, Manuel Sherman, John Stultz, and Joe Arrellano. *Front row:* H. J. Robinson, John Fisher, Justice of the Peace John Burke, Thomas Smith, Charles Stultz, Captain Henry J. Nelson, James Sheehan, Frank Charles, Myron Breckenridge, Fred Klein, and Joseph Boyd. After Concord was incorporated in 1905 the upper floor of the firehouse was used as the city hall.

The firehouse was moved to Willow Pass Road between Galindo and Mount Diablo Streets in 1911 to make way for construction of the first Concord Inn. It was moved again a few years ago, for the benefit of the Bank of America, to Galindo Street, near Salvio. It has had several uses over the years, serving as a chamber of commerce office at two different times, and as Salvation Army headquarters, and as a place of business.

Barney Believed in Advertising

Judging by the sign he is leaning against, Bernhardt "Barney" Neustadter was promotion minded. This was his general store on Salvio Street, Concord, as it appeared in the 1880s. Barney's son, Mitch, is in the left foreground with one leg crossed in front of the other. The girl is Mitch's sister, Jeanette. The Neustadter family had come to Concord from Nortonville. Their store was on the south side of Salvio Street between Mount Diablo and Galindo Streets. A machine shop, which did a brisk business making and repairing farm implements was just down the street to the west. Other businesses on the street included Paul Keller's hardware store, Henry Ivey's livery stable, the Klein Hotel, Navas & Beebe store and the Randall Brothers' general store.

Concord Was Site Of County Fairs

WITH completion of the pavilion at the County Fair Grounds in 1861, Concord became the locale for many exciting events and celebrations. There were rodeos, fiestas, harness races, and—of course—parades. The fair grounds were located north of the Pacheco-Concord road, not far from the site of the present Buchanan Airport. The fair was held here every summer from 1861 through the early 1900's. The ladies being reviewed in this photo may have been from the Grange or one of the lodges that enriched the town's social life. The year's biggest celebration, however, was held in the plaza that Salvio Pacheco had donated to Concord: a Fourth of July barbecue and parade.

The Wedding of Marina Amador And Juan Galindo

Marina Amador was the prettiest young woman in the new town of Concord. She had dark eyes and long dark hair and a friendly outgoing manner. Her mother had died when she was a girl. Her father, Vicente Amador, had remarried and moved away, and so Marina lived with her grandfather, Salvio Pacheco, in a big adobe home that had been built many years before.

Marina's favorite suitor was her cousin, Juan Crisostomo Galindo, son of Don Francisco. Their courtship is unrecorded by historians, but they must have had wonderful times together, picnicking and horseback riding in the great open Diablo Valley—all under the watchful eyes of a dueña, of course. The valley had rolling grass-covered hills, and many large wheat farms. There were giant oaks, streams filled with fish, and very few fences, roads, or houses.

Marina and Juan were descended from Spanish families whose names are important in the history of California: Pacheco, Bernal, Flores, Amador, and Galindo. Juan's father started the posh Galindo Hotel in Oakland and was one of the wealthiest men in the state, owning ranches and other real estate in Alameda and Contra Costa Counties.

Marina and Juan were married on Wednesday, July 23, 1873, in their grandfather's adobe. Their wedding picture is shown here. After the marriage ceremony a big celebration was held that lasted for many days. Guests came from all over California. Many of them pitched tents near the adobe and camped out during the wedding fiesta. There were dances every night and many daytime events, including horse races, rodeos, bull fights, card games, and barbecues.

The newlyweds moved into the Galindo family home, which still stands on Amador Street in Concord. Juan (later called John) Galindo became a member of the Concord school board and later served as a county supervisor. Several of the Galindos' children and grandchildren continued the family tradition of public service in various civic, official, and teaching positions. Many descendants of Marina and John Galindo still live in Concord.

These Two Buildings--A Hotel and A Bakery--Served Concord For Many Years

The first hotel in Concord was started by Philip Klein in 1870 on the northeast corner of Salvio and Mount diablo Streets, facing the plaza. It was later owned by Joe DeRosa. The hotel is shown above as it looked in 1901.

John Lambert's Bakery building was a colorful example of do-it-yourself architecture. Five generations of Concord citizens enjoyed the imaginative arches and decorative effects lovingly constructed brick-by-brick in 1884. The sketch at left was made by artist Dick Weber for Mr. and Mrs. Guido Ginochio, who had owned the **octogenarian** building before it was torn down in 1967.

Both of these historic buildings were victims of real estate developers and city bureaucrats, who managed to destroy several priceless landmarks in the late 1960s.

Trains Brought Mail and Passengers, Carried Crops to Markets

Southern Pacific built many depots like this one all over the West. This one was near the present site of Market Street, opposite Concord Shopping Center. The photo was taken in the early 1900s. A horse and wagon is there to meet the train. As you can see, women were still burdened by the voluminous fashions of the late Victorian era. The railroad carried mail, passengers, and freight. Trains were especially important to local farmers, who shipped crops by rail to markets many miles away. The Concord station was part of Southern Pacific's San Ramon Valley branch line. A local passenger and freight train left Oakland every morning and looped through Contra Costa and Alameda Counties. The train passed through Richmond, turned off the main line at Martinez and then traveled through Avon, Concord, Walnut Creek, Alamo, and Danville to San Ramon. Then it went to Pleasanton and steamed down Niles Canyon and back to Oakland.

High school classes were originally held in the grammar school building and Odd Fellows Hall until Mount Diablo High School, shown above, was built in 1905.

Main Street, Concord, Cal.

This is Salvio Street, looking east from the Galindo Street intersection in 1908. On the right (from front to back) is J.J. January's Concord Drug Store, the post office, Union Saloon, the office of John J. Buche (justice of the peace), another saloon, the Neustaider store, Wiecker's Mt. Diablo Hotel, and Mrs. Henry Nelson's millinery store.

SCENES OF CONCOR

Photographers and artists provided us with these glimpses of the pasto setting of Concord in the era between 1900 and 1910: scenes that ha disappeared from Contra Costa County. Like most towns in the cou during this era, Concord served the needs of farmers, who came to tow

Wheat was being harvested at the Foskett & Elworthy ranch on the east side of Cocord. The site of this ranch is now covered with ranch-style homes

Here is the Randall Brothers' store, on the southwest corner of Salvio Street and Galindo Street. Edward and Samuel Randall did a brisk business selling general merchandise from 1883 to 1911. Concord's first telephone exchange was also in this building. A public reading room—the beginning of a library—was in the building at right.

N THE EARLY 1900s

uy tools and supplies—and to exchange gossip with friends. The pan-rama below is reproduced from double post cards published for C.W. lein, a Concord druggist. The vantage point is at Clayton Road near the lameda. Queen of All Saints Church can be seen in the background.

Here Comes the Big Parade!

Concord had a two-day Independence celebration in 1909, with harness races at the Concord race track on July 4th and a big parade on Monday, the 5th, sponsored by Wahoo Tribe No. 194, International Order of Red Men. The Concord Silver Band is marching down Salvio Street, opposite the plaza, followed by the Odd Fellows and a patriotic float. "The Place," in the middle of the photo, was a favorite tavern. The lower photo shows a view of the same location on a busy shopping day in 1937. The businesses shown include Mac's Tavern, operated by L.B. McKinnon; Klein's Drug Store; Concord Hotel (formerly Klein's Hotel); the Coffee Cup; Williamson's Fountain, Tony's Toggery, and Mangini's Drugs. The latter store continued well into the 1960s. There are many old-timers who remember Louis Mangini personally preparing prescriptions and waiting on his customers.

Historic Odd Fellows Hall Survived for Nearly a Century, Then It Was Destroyed by Indifferent Bureacrats

The Odd Fellows Hall was one of the social centers of Concord for nearly 100 years. Pacheco Lodge No. 117 and Mount Diablo Rebekah Lodge No. 228 of the Independent Order of Odd Fellows met in this building, as did two junior lodges of the order. The First Presbyterian Church across the street used it for a Sunday school and other church groups held services in the building at various times. Many local organizations had pot luck dinners, meetings, parties, and rummage sales in it. The lodge building also housed legal and real estate offices in the 1940s, '50s, and '60s.

Lodge No. 117 was started in Pacheco on September 12, 1863. Some noteworthy Contra Costa pioneers served as officers in the early years of the lodge, including Paul Shirley, W.T. Hendrick, L.B. Farish, John Gambs, J.H. Carothers, E. Hook, William Gieraw, W.A. Smith, and G.W. Johnson. A meeting hall errected in 1871 was destroyed by fire the same year. A new bigger hall was built of redwood lumber by lodge members in 1872. J.P. Munro-Fraser, an eminent historian, described that hall as "one of the most elegant buildings to be found in all California." Of eclectic design, it had an arched entrance and arched windows in the front.

The building was moved from Pacheco to Salvio and Colfax Streets, Concord, in 1893, using huge rollers and a team of horses. Because the building was often mired in mud along the way, the moving operation took three months. The first mover to attempt the job had quit and the job was successfully completed by a company run by a woman, long before women had the right to vote, let alone worry about the Equal Rights Amendment.

The photograph shows the historic building in the mid 1950s. Downtown Concord had grown up around it. Parking problems had begun to afflict the city. The trustees of the Presbyterian church were looking for more parking spaces for their members. They looked across the street and coveted the property of their neighbors, the Odd Fellows.

The church people did not care much one way or another about the architectural qualities of the lodge building or about its historical importance. Their priority was parking. If they could just get ahold of the property and tear down the lodge building, they would have a parking lot. One of their members was Farrell A. "Bud" Stewart, the city manager. And thus it happened in 1969 that the city building inspectors found, after nearly 100 years, that the lodge hall had some technical building code violations. Despite a public outcry to save the structure, the city bureaucrats prevailed and the building was destroyed. The I.O.O.F. Hall was so strong that it took much longer to wreck it than most other buildings of similar size. It must be said, lest Bud Stewart and the church get all the blame, that the Odd Fellows of 1969 were not the same kind of tough pioneers as the Odd Fellows of a hundred years before. Those old pioneers would have fought tooth and nail before they would let a bunch of people in swivel chairs take away the hall they built. No sir. These modern Odd Fellows had lost the pioneer spirit. They just let the city and the church take their building, with hardly a whimper-- and then they took the "pieces of silver" from the church in exchange for a priceless historic heritage.

The Presbyterians now use the site as a parking lot. And they do not forgive any tresspasses, but have offending vehicles towed away.

Concord's First Luxury Hotel, Built in 1911

Concord provided rest and refreshment for the weary traveler with a number of unpretentious hotels, but the city marked a turning point in 1911 with construction of the luxurious Concord Inn, facing the plaza. It had impressive Grecian columns at the entrance. There was a roof garden, and each of the 64 rooms had a telephone. It was designed by prominent architect W.H. Weeks. Flanking it on Mount Diablo Street were the post office and Concord Mercantile Company. In 1917 the entire block burned down in one of the city's worst fires. In 1958 another Concord Inn was built on Willow Pass Road. This one lasted till the 1980s, when it was torn down to make room for an office building which was errected on the site.

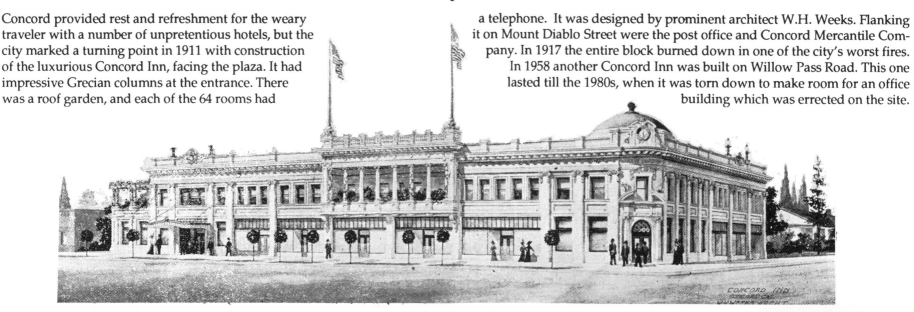

Bacon Block Housed Newspaper, Ice Cream Parlor, and Bakery

The Bacon Block on Mount Diablo Street was built in 1914 by Webster and Mary Bacon, who came to Concord from Crow's Landing. A large building was often called a "block" in those days. When this picture was taken, in 1915, the building was occupied by Parker's Ice Cream Parlor and Stationery Store; the *Concord Transcript*, published by Catherine Burke; Bacon's Grocery, and Graham Bakery. There were apartments upstairs. At the extreme left background you can see part of the Bank of Concord in the next block (which burned down along with the Concord Inn and Concord Mercantile in 1917). The building next door was Klein's Drugs, later Mac's Tavern, owned by L.B. McKinnon, and still later The Old Hangout. The Bacon Block was remodeled by Michael Gourkani in the mid-1970s. The ground floor was then occupied by Hobie's Roadhouse Restaurant and the Mount Diablo Therapy Center Thrift Shop. Incidentally—after a long time in other locations—the *Concord Transcript* offices moved back into this building a year or two ago, this time as part of Lesher Communications. This photo was contributed by Genevieve Norton, who used to live in an apartment in the Bacon Block.

Mount Diablo High School Football Team, 1912

Student representatives of four high schools met in Martinez in 1903 to form an interscholastic athletic association. The association was reorganized in 1908 to include all high schools in the area: Liberty, Alhambra, John Swett, Riverview, and Mount Diablo. The first interscholastic sports were tennis, baseball, and track. Football started in 1909. From its first undefeated season that year Mount Diablo's football team had an enviable won-lost record. Pictured above is one of the school's mighty early teams, the team of 1912. *Standing, left to right:* Arden Randall, Ralph West, Elwin Williams, Clark Leh (team captain), Mylo Lee, the coach (whose name is unremembered), and Arlo Sperry. *Kneeling, left to right:* John Barber, Wayman Ballenger (who became city clerk), Roy Bibber, Herbert Elworthy, and Raymond Sawyer. This photo came from Charlotte Ballenger, beloved former teacher, widow of Wayman, and daughter of Concord's first mayor.

The Day It Snowed in Concord: January 9, 1913

It snowed in Concord on January 9, 1913. Somebody got a camera and took a picture of Saloonkeeper Francisco Perez with three of his customers out in front of his saloon on the southwest corner of Grant Street and Willow Pass Road. The snow on the ground was already melting, but the tree branches and roof tops were still covered. It wasn't much snowfall to an Easterner, but for Concord it was a blizzard. The saloon advertised Brooklyn Steam Beer for 5 cents a glass with a poster affixed to a tree. Concord was just a small country town in 1913, even though it had been incorporated as a city in 1905. However, the Oakland, Antioch, and Eastern Railway (forerunner to BART) started in 1912, bringing the first wave of commuters to Concord– a hint of times to come. The saloon, later owned by Allen Vargas, continued for many years. The building was torn down in 1955 to be replaced by an office of American Trust Company (now Wells Fargo Bank).

Telephone Operators Knew Everybody's Number

"Number please" was what you heard when you picked up your telephone in Concord during the halcyon days before the dial system went into effect. Along with Martinez, Danville, and several other towns, Concord got its first telephone service in 1881. Actually each town only had one telephone that first year—at its respective Southern Pacific station. The railroad had installed the phones mostly for its own use. The first telephone exchange was started in Martinez in 1907, with other towns following soon after. The photo shows the Concord exchange in February 1916. The women are, left to right, Chief Operator Edith Bolla; a relief operator (name not known), and three regular operators—Amanda Sibrian, Florence Vargas, and Eva Fiske. The two switchboards can be seen at left. The

telephone exchange was first located in Randall Brothers' general store, Galindo and Salvio Streets. In a few years the switchboards, wires, desks, and operators moved across the street to the second floor of the Foskett and Elworthy Building, above the First National Bank, which is where they were when this photo was taken. (Incidently, the Foskett and Elworthy Building has been restored, fortunately, through the efforts of Aldo Vasconi and Fred Doster.) There were just over 300 phones in Concord in 1916. The operators knew most of the numbers; if a caller didn't know a number, a friendly operator would still get the caller connected. The exchange received about 150 calls per day. In 1940 the same two switchboards were still in use, still receiving about the same number of calls.

Everyone Met at Willie's in the '20s and '30s . . .

Williamson's Fountain was a popular hangout in downtown Concord in the 1920s and '30s. Behind the counter are P.M. "Willie" Williamson, the proprietor, and Gladys Williams, a soda jerk and daughter of the city librarian. Willie's wife, Mae, and his daughter, Wilma, also worked at the fountain. Tobacco and candy counters are at the right; the booths were way in the back. Willie's place served hot meals, sandwiches, and homemade ice cream. The walls were decorated with pictures of Mount Diablo, painted by Charles S. Adams. The fountain was on Salvio Street facing the plaza, in the same building as Tony's Toggery and Mangini's Drugs. A generation later it was the Sun & Moon Restaurant and then the Sandwich Factory. The building was torn down by the Concord Redevelopment Agency in 1981 and replaced by a huge Mission-Revival style building.

. . . and at Mr. B's Fountain in the '50s

When you went shopping in Concord in the 1950s, Mr. B's Fountain was where you stopped for a break. If you were a teenager, it was where you went after school. You got a three-scoop ice cream sundae for 39 cents and a cherry coke for a dime. More than one romance had its beginning over a shared ice cream soda at Mr. B's. The photo shows the fountain when it opened on June 10, 1949, as part of Aldo Vasconi's Concord Drug Store on Salvio Street. The lady seated at the counter is Sylvia Vasconi, Aldo's wife. Behind the ccounter are Ellen Sanders Donahue, wearing a "New Look" dress, and Lenny Brazil, "Mr. B" himself.

Mount Diablo Hospital Started in a Bungalow

Winton G. Blackwell

Edna Haywood, a registered nurse in Concord, went to work for Dr. Henry W. Stirewalt in 1927, traveling around Contra Costa County attending to the sick. In 1930, at Dr. Stirewalt's urging, she took over the lease of a bungalow on East Street, Concord, that was being used as a convalescent hospital. And then, with a $7,500 loan from her father-in-law, she bought the bungalow and had it remodeled to become the new six-bed Concord Hospital. During the first few years Mrs. Haywood and her husband lived in the basement of the hospital because they couldn't afford a separate home. Mrs. Haywood recalled, "I had to be the business manager, dietitian, director of nurses, and head surgical nurse. I took care of the laundry, and at night when the patients were asleep I would iron all the sheets for the next day." A tank house in the backyard of the house was converted into an operating room. The original Concord Hospital is shown at left in the above photo. In 1935 the two-story

building in back was added, providing 10 more beds, a surgery room, emergency room, and offices. This building had the first elevator in Concord. In 1947 Mrs. Haywood sold the hospital to a doctor who sold it again two years later to a new non-profit corporation. In 1952 the hospital came into public ownership under the aegis of the Concord-Pleasant Hill Hospital District. An outstanding adminisistrator of the institution was Winton G. Blackwell, who took over in 1951 when the hospital had 30 beds and 71 employees. He oversaw the addition of two new buildings during his 17-year tenure. When he retired the hospital had 195 beds and 600 employees. The name was changed to Mount Diablo Hospital in 1972. It has grown considerably since then. In the 1980s the hospital was involved in a long, bitter controversy over private or public ownership, which fortunately was resolved with the institution continuing in public ownership.

Memorable Retailers of Concord

There have been many. Here are some that are especially noteworthy:

CONCORD MERCANTILE (above left): In 1911, when people needed shoes, dishes, groceries, or whatever, they looked first in the Concord Mercantile store. Frederick Galindo, the owner, is behind the counter at left. The store had two entrances—on Mount Diablo Street and on Salvio Street.

SATTLER'S (above right): That's Ernie Sattler in front of his appliance workshop, which he had just opened in 1937 in an old tankhouse on Concord Boulevard, two miles east of town. He was joined in the business by his younger brothers, Hank and Bill in 1945. The trio remodeled a building that had housed Eddie's Garage on Willow Pass Road and thus started an appliance business that served Contra Costa for half of a century, with Hank's son, Dennis taking over the helm later.

BEEDE'S (below right): Concord's popular variety store, run by Roy and Betty Beede, shown here during the big flood of April 1958. Employees were sweeping water out for days. With an admittedly ungrammatical slogan—"If Beede's don't have it, you don't need it"—the store endeared itself to two generations of

customers. The Quality Bakery and the jewelry store were likewise popular stops on a downtown shopping trip, and have continued in business under new owners.

FARM BUREAU MARKET (left) was really out in the country when it was started over a half century ago at Farm Bureau Road and Walnut Avenue. Now it is the oldest country store in Concord, but the city surrounds it.

Cowell Cement Plant Is Gone, But Smokestack Remains

The Cowell Cement Plant, world's largest, was founded in 1908 by Henry Cowell, who later gave it to his son, Samuel. Workers in the plant were for the most part required to live in the nearby village of Cowell--and to buy their groceries and other necessities from the company store, at outrageously high prices, with the amounts of their purchases deducted from their paychecks. The plant made the Cowell family rich, but it was a nuisance to nearby Concord farmers because it spewed white caustic dust into the air, which settled on their crops. The plant management refused to abate the dust. The farmers sued and lost. Finally, in 1933, a young lawyer named John Garaventa took the farmers' case. After a 53-day trial the judge ordered the cement company to put dust collectors on each of its eight vent chimneys and Garaventa became a public hero--the Ralph Nader of his day.

The cement plant continued in business until 1947, when the workers went on strike and the management decided to close the plant rather than meet the employees' terms. The old plant and the nearby village became an artists's colony, with many craft shops and a wallpaper factory. The old Cowell hospital became a childcare center. There was a huge tree with a deluxe treehouse out in back. Later this building had a picture frame shop in front and a newspaper office in back, leased by the author of this book, who remembers pleasant moments of relaxation sitting in the treehouse. The cement plant and the village were torn down in the early 1970s to make way for a new housing subdivision, now part of Concord. The smokestack and the village firehouse were kept as landmarks. John Garaventa became Concord's first municipal judge, serving in the 1950s and '60s.

Coast-toCoast First Flight

First!

The beginning of commercial avaiation, as we know it today, took place in Concord, California, on September 1, 1927. A Boeing 40-B2 took off and headed east while hundreds of Concord citizens and people from all over California watched. The plane flew at 150 miles per hour. Two passengers, with mail and other cargo, were landed in New York 12 hours later. *This was the first coast-to-coast commercial passenger flight.* The plane belonged to Boeing Air Transport, which later became United Airlines. The historic site of the takeoff was a small airport off West Street, between Concord Boulevard and Clayton Road. It had been built by the army after World War I. Soon after giving Concord a special place in aviation history, Boeing moved its operations to larger metropolitan airports. The small field in Concord was used by private pilots in the 1930s. It fell into disuse in the 1940s after the opening of Sherman Field in Pleasant Hill and then Buchanan Field on the other side of Concord. The former runways are now covered with homes. The old airplane hanger remained standing through the mid-1980s, just across from the Methodist Church on West Street. In the 1940s and '50s the old brick hanger building was used as a factory by Niagara Duplicating Machine Company. And then it was occupied by the John Burton Machine Corporation until 1975. After standing empty for more than a decade it was torn down and new homes were built on the site. Sherman Field is also now covered with homes, but every once in a while a home owner there starts digging in his backyard and discovers a chunk of tarmac from the old landing strip.

County Airport Started in 1942
It Became an Army Field During World War II, And Then Reverted to County Ownership

Supervisor Billy Buchanan got a kiss during dedication ceremonies for Buchanan Field. It was named for him to honor his 40 years of service to the county.

Back in the 1920s and 1930s barnstorming airplane pilots would often land in pastures. There were only two notable airfields in Contra Costa county: Sherman Field in Pleasant Hill and the small field on West Street in Concord mentioned on the previous page. Much earlier there had been a tiny airfield along East Street in Concord.

A citizens' committee headed by Richmond industrialist Fred D. Parr chose a site for the county airport--407 acres between Concord and Pacheco, bought by the Board of Supervisors in 1942. The field was used by the U.S. Army Air Corps during World War II as an advanced training base for P-39 Aircobra pilots. The Army added 122 acres to the field, extended the runways, and built additional taxiways.

In 1946 the field was returned to county control. Dedication ceremonies were held August 4, 1946, sponsored by the Contra Costa County Development Association. The airport was named after the beloved long-time chairman of the Board of Supervisors, William J. "Billy" Buchanan. About 15,000 people came to the dedication program, which featured demonstrations of formation flying by military pilots and stunt flying by private pilots. The Richmond Municipal Band and Camp Stoneman Army Band performed and a plaque was presented to Supervisor Buchanan by his grandson.

A new control tower was built in 1960. Additional runways and navigation equipment have been added since then. Buchanan Field has become one of the 20 busiest airports in the United States.

LEFT:: *This is how the tower and administration building looked in 1950. The building was pretty nice for a small airport, with a lounge for passengers and pilots and "state-of-the-art" for-its-time electronic equipment in the tower and on the roof.*

RIGHT: *Marvin Scott was airport manager from 1950 to 1977. Most of the growth of the field was achieved during his administration. He resigned because of a dispute with his boss, public works director Vernon Cline, a bureaucrat who knew little about airport management, but interfered constantly with Scott's decisions.*

Marvin Scott

Chapter 11

Pleasant Hill School Started Long Before the Town

A lot of children would like to attend a school like this one. Why put up with fenced asphalt-paved schoolyards when you could be in a grove of eucalyptus trees, surrounded by orchards and dairy farms? And who wouldn't like to ride a pony to school, as many kids did in 1918, when this photo was taken of the Pleasant Hill School. Of course, it was primitive. Water came from a well--and the toilet was outdoors--but that just added to the rural charm. And, besides, classes were held for only three or four months a year. The Pleasant Hill School was named for a nearby hill, which had been named by a surveyor in 1852. There had been two other schools in the Pleasant Hill district before this one: the first was just a large room in a house and had started in 1866; the other was a tiny one-room school-house that had been built about 1874. The school shown above started in 1912 with the construction of the two-room building at left; the addition in back was built in 1917 and had just one large room, which was used variously as an assembly room, gymnasium, or classroom. The kids in this informal photo seem to be enjoying themselves—sitting under the trees and hanging out on the porch—with the exception of the boy with a mop and bucket on the porch at left. Pupils were expected to help with school maintenance chores in those days. This school was replaced by another larger one in 1920 and there have been many more schools built in the district since, especially after the town of Pleasant Hill was started in the late 1940s.

Pleasant Hill Was All Farmland until the 1940s

The place that became Pleasant Hill was part of the only "gringo" land grant in Contra Costa County, Rancho Las Juntas, given to an Irishman, William Welch, in 1844. Welch and his family lived in Pueblo de San Jose until 1845, when they moved to the rancho. Welch died the next year, leaving his widow and nine children with the rancho to take care of. Mrs. Welch (a sister of Francisco Galindo), and the children, who were grown, sold off much of the land to various American settlers, including William Hook, Patrick Rodgers, David Boss, F.M. Warmcastle, and John Hazeltine, who started farms in the area which eventually became Pleasant Hill but remained as farmland for 100 years. The countryside was covered with wheat fields, vineyards, and orchards. The photo shows a farmers' market at the intersection of two highways, later known as North Main Street and Boyd Road, in the autumn of 1921. The farmers were offering fresh squash, grapes, pumpkins, and jars of home-made preserves. A large wooden sign at the busy intersection gave directions to various communities along the road. The Soldiers' Monument, erected after World War I, stands near the place where the farmers' market used to be. In 1949 Gregory Gardens (with houses selling for $7,950 to $8,950) became the first subdivision in what later became the city of Pleasant Hill. The last farm here, some 82 acres, known as the "Cabbage Patch," was owned by Dr. Lathrop Ellinwood for nearly 65 years. It was developed as a planned community in the late 1980s.

139

The County's First Junior College Was Started in Pleasant Hill

The Contra Costa Junior College District was established December 14, 1948, with a governing board of five members elected by the public. Diablo Valley College was started by the district in 1950. At first, classes were held in various school rooms in Martinez. The college moved to its new campus on Golf Club Road, Pleasant Hill, in 1952, beginning with temporary buildings. The campus is shown in the mid 1960s, when most of the main buildings had been completed. The pond in the foreground has attracted many ducks. Watching—and sometimes feeding—the ducks has become a pleasant diversion for students and instructors strolling or sitting by the pond during lunchtime or between classes. The college offers both academic and vocational programs. It's dental technician courses and hotel and restaurant division are outstanding. DVC offers programs for the community too, including an arts and lectures series, film series, workshops, and forums. The planetarium, science center, and museum are open to the public. Associate in Arts degrees are offered in Apparel Design, Business, Dental Hygiene, Electronics, Police Science, Vocational Nursing, and other subjects. A large majority of each graduating class has transferred to four-year colleges. The district, now called Contra Costa Community College District, has established two other similar colleges--Contra Costa College in San Pablo and Los Medanos College in Pittsburg. The name *Los Medanos* comes from the original name of the land grant on which Pittsburg is situated. It means *sand dunes*.

Rowboats Were Needed in Gregory Gardens

As mentioned on a previous page, the flood of April 1958 was one of the worst in county history. Here is an aerial view of the Gregory Gardens tract in Pleasant Hill, looking northeast, taken by Russ Reed. Streets and yards were under water; rowboats would have been a handy mode of transportation. All of these homes were built low to the ground on concrete slab foundations; many residents had interior floors covered by water. The nearby Cherry Lane area was even worse: hip-deep in water. And Broadway Shopping Center in Walnut Creek looked like Venice. Levees in the Delta began to give way. Sheriff's deputies, police officers, and hundreds of Civil Defense volunteers carried sandbags to the levees, shoveled mud from streets, and rescued residents trapped in their homes. Schools were used as temporary shelters for some flood victims. After several years of study the Army Corps of Engineers proposed a $9 million flood-control project to be paid for mostly by the federal government. By that time the weather had been dry for a time and some local property owners wanted to delay the project. However, wiser heads eventually prevailed. Many drainage improvements have been completed and a disaster like the flood of 1958 is not expected to occur again.

Bay Point (Port Chicago)
Started as a Lumber Mill Town

In 1907 the C.A. Smith Lumber Company bought 1,500 acres of riverfront land about five miles east of Martinez and started a lumber finishing mill, the biggest on the Pacific Coast. The mill was located near deep-water docks, where raw lumber was received from the company's headquarters in Coos Bay, Oregon. The town of Bay Point grew up around this mill. The first retail establishment was a general store started by William Smith of Pittsburg, and the first two homes were built by William Buholtz and Samuel Gilroy, all in 1908. An Odd Fellows hall and a movie theatre were built in 1911 and the California Hotel was built in 1916. Many families in the new town were of Scandinavian descent, with names like Peterson, Cunningham, Erickson, and Fagerstrom. They had traveled with the lumber company from Oregon.

After a fire in 1913 the mill was rebuilt and the company was reorganized as the Coos Bay Lumber Company. In 1917 Pacific Coast Shipbuilding Company started a shipyard at Bay Point to build 10,000-ton freighters for the Allied war effort. After the war the shipyards closed down.

The railroad station at Bay Point, pictured above, was one of the busiest in the country. Thousands of carloads of lumber products were shipped from this station to customers all over the United States.

The Royal Hotel and Restaurant (above left) featured a daily "Royal Lunch" popular with mill workers.

Everybody in town went to the Liberty Star Theatre, pictured below left as it looked in 1932, when a Will Rogers movie was being shown.

A casualty of the Depression, the lumber mill went back to Oregon in 1932, leaving many unemployed workers behind. The name of the town was changed to Port Chicago as part of a promotion to attract new industry. The promotion was somewhat successful and many people went back to work.

Navy Caused Worst Disaster in County History

The Port Chicago Naval Magazine was established "temporarily" in 1942 to ship munitions to Pacific area battle zones during World War 2.

The negligence of the commanding officer and his subordinates caused a terrible disaster on Monday, July 17, 1944. One transport ship was moored at a Navy pier, waiting to be loaded with bombs and ammunition from railroad cars parked on the pier. A second ship was on the other side of the pier, already loaded. Two explosions came at 10:18 p.m., about two seconds apart, according to earthquake measuring devices in Berkeley. A wave of water 20 to 30 feet high swept down the river, destroying a Coast Guard vessel and an oil tanker. The latter was fortunately empty.

All persons within 1,000 feet of the blast were killed. There were many serious injuries to civilians and military people outside that perimeter. Of the dead, 202 were Navy enlisted men of the loading crews, mostly African-Americans. At this munitions dump African-Americans were given the most menial and most hazardous jobs. Also dead were 9 officers of the loading crews, 5 men aboard a fireboat, 3 civilian train crewmen, 3 construction company employees, a 30-man guard detail, and 67 officers and men aboard the two ships. Windows were shattered in Oakland and Petaluma and there was structural damage to buildings in Fairfield, Vallejo, and every town and city in Contra Costa County.

There were more people killed in this 1944 explosion and more property damaged than in all other disasters in the history of the county put together.

The photo at left shows the splintered remains of the pier after the explosion.

In the mid-1950s Congressman John F. Baldwin, directors of the Contra Costa County Development Association, and several county officials launched an all-out effort to get the Navy base moved away from Contra Costa, citing the dangers of trucks, trains, and ships laden with explosive materials. In 1958 the Board of Pilot Commissioners joined the effort, pointing out that more than 500 oil tankers used the same channel as the munitions ships. Just one collision would kill thousands of people in Concord, Martinez, Pleasant Hill, and Pittsburg. In 1967 the *Contra Costa Times* ran a four-part series of articles by Robert A. Neuman, a senior editor, on "The Case for Moving the Navy."

But, like the 500-pound gorilla who sits where he wants, the Navy did not want to move—and didn't.

Citizens Rebuilt Their Town, Then The Navy Destroyed it Again

The Navy paid an average of $1,300 each for the 300 homes ruined by the blast, a paltry sum even then. But the people rebuilt their town. The photo at right shows Port Chicago as it looked in 1953. The then-recently completed school can be seen at right. Behind the school is Las Lomitas, a new residential development. The main business street runs diagonally near the center of the picture. There were two gas stations, a hardware store, a pharmacy, a market, a theatre, and several other businesses. It was a small friendly community of home owners, where everybody knew everybody else. The town's most famous resident, former 49er and Saint Danny Colchico, was on a first-name basis with his neighbors.

When you look at this placid scene it's hard to realize that by the mid-1960s the town was in turmoil. The munitions dump, renamed Concord Naval Weapons Station, was the major shipping point for bombs to Vietnam. Antiwar protestors held frequent demonstrations near the Navy docks, future congressman George Miller being among them. With an administration in Washington hypersensitive to critcism, the decision was made to keep the demonstrators away by eliminating the town.

In 1969 Pentagon officials petitioned to have the town condemned as a "buffer zone." An elderly, possibly senile federal judge went along with the Navy lawyers in spite of facts that totally contradicted the Navy's case.

The Navy evicted the population, bulldozed or moved all the buildings, and ringed the site with barbed wire and armed guards. A whole town was gone forever.

Clyde, the Unique "Rainbow City"

The Clyde Hotel, shown as it looked about 1920, was the focal point of the village of Clyde, built during World War I to house workers from the nearby Pacific Coast Shipyard at Bay Point. The town and hotel had already been planned by architects E.W. Cannon and G.A. Applegarth when Bernard Maybeck, the famous designer of San Francisco's Palace of Fine Arts, was hired as consulting architect. Maybeck changed the gridiron pattern of the streets to one with gently curving roads adapted to the hillside site. He varied setbacks of the houses to provide better exposures and views. He also improved the three-story hotel design, which featured Spanish Rennaisance exterior decorations. Maybeck created a striking interior with tall piers in the lobby. A wooden frieze near the ceiling was ornamented with band-sawn shapes. Applegarth had been trained at Ecole des Beaux Arts and welcomed Maybeck's ideas. There were 120 homes built in the village in 1918, painted in a variety of pastel colors: baby blue, lavender, yellow, and pink. Clyde thus acquired its nickname, "Rainbow City." The shipyards closed after the war and the village was nearly deserted until 1932 when it was bought by Walter and Eunice VanWinkle. To lure tenants the VanWinkles rented the homes for only $20 a month. The hotel at various times served as a government hospital, headquarters for the Civilian Conservation Corps, and as housing for 117 guards hired in the 1930s to protect neighboring oil refineries. The hotel burned to the ground in 1969. Eventually the 120 original houses, plus a few built later, were purchased by individual owners. The unique village still stands, its three curving streets serving as a memento of Maybeck, one of America's greatest architects.

Bernard Maybeck, circa 1930

144

Chapter 12

Brentwood Started as Center of a Vast Agricultural Empire

The San Pablo & Tulare Railroad established a depot in Brentwood in 1878 on a corner of the huge old rancho once owned by John Marsh. Gruneacur's General Store and Joe Carey's Bllacksmith Shop were started near the depot, followed within a few years by several dozen houses and business firms, all clustered around the depot. Thousands of tons of produce from East County farms were shipped from this depot.

Brentwood entered the Twentieth Century with a bang when a big Scottish-owned agricultural firm, Balfour, Guthrie & Company, bought virtually the entire former Marsh rancho for about $200,000. Balfour-Guthrie built the Brentwood

Hotel near the depot for use as executive offices and to house some of the firm's employees. Architecturally the hotel combined Classical and Mission Revival features, with arches and columns gracing the ground floor. This 1913 photo shows Balfour-Guthrie's survey crew posing for a picture in front of the hotel. There is a list of names written on the border of the original photo, but there are fewer names on the list than people in the picture, so we are not sure who is who. Here are the names as they were written: 1. _____. 2. (Mrs.?) Wooley. 3. Kempe. 4. Bill Wooley. 5. Joe Vance. 6. Ray Goddwin. 7. Dick Wallace. 8. Rob. 9. Bing Maloney. 10. _____. 11. Pete Mecrill. 12. Geo. Shafer. 13. Jerry Jones.

Irrigation Project Was Started in 1913

Farming has always been important in East County—and the supply of fresh water is crucial. In 1913 a major irrigation project was started by the East Contra Costa Irrigation Company, a mutual organization of farmers, financed mainly by Balfour-Guthrie. The irrigation company was later taken over by the Knightsen, Lone Tree, and Brentwood Irrigation Districts, which in turn were later combined into a larger district. Balfour-Guthrie, by far the largest land holder, with some 13,000 acres of the former Marsh property, planted huge orchards, shipping fresh fruit all over the United States and dried fruit all over the world until the mid 1940s.

After 80 years the irrigation system is still in use. The flow of water from the Sacramento River is now controlled by the Shasta Dam, which helps prevent intrusion of salt water into the system. The Sacramento River water is diverted between Locke and Walnut Grove through the Cross-Delta Canal into the Mokelumne River, then into the San Joaquin River, where federal and state pumps export Delta water to thieving real estate developers in Southern California. The Delta irrigation system consists of seven pumping stations, lifting water in successive stages to a maximum of 144 feet, distributing water to farms and orchards at each level. The main canal and laterals, all lined with concrete, were constructed in 1913, '14, and '15. The photo shows the historic beginning of this work, the dredger *Samson* digging the canal from Indian Slough to the first pumping station in 1913.

Irrigated Orchards Produced Huge Crops

Peaches, pears, apricots, and cherries from Brentwood were of exceptionally high quality. Balfour-Guthrie people were dedicated to proper care of their trees, which included irrigation, tilling the soil, fertilizing—and probably some love.

The photo at left shows Charles B. Weeks, Sr., supervising the application of irrigation water to an orchard.

Balfour-Guthrie pioneered the use of airplanes to spray and dust orchards to control insect pests.

As an example of results, the yield of peaches in Balfour-Guthrie orchards averaged more than ten tons per acre, far above the yield realized elsewhere.

World's Largest Drying Yard

The photo at right shows some of the 36,000 trays filled with Lovell & Muir peaches in Balfour-Guthrie's drying yard—the largest in the world. A few weeks earlier the same trays were filled with apricots drying in the sun. Later bartlett pears and stanwick nectarines were dried. Hundreds of men and women were employed. The cutting and packing shed had special equipment for washing boxes, scraping trays, etc.

The company even had its own little railroad to transport fruit where needed. After the cut fruit was placed on drying trays, the trays were stacked on narrow-gauge rail cars and moved into the sulphur treating sheds. After the sulphur treatment, the cars took the fruit to the drying yard.

Balfour-Guthrie Harvest Crews Lived in Small Cottages and Barracks

At harvest time many hundreds of extra workers were needed on Balfour-Guthrie orchards. The company provided barracks and tents for single men; small cottages for families. They weren't grand, but they were clean and decent, better than the facilities found at many other farms. Some of the children of workers and the workers themselves are shown in the photo. The man with a white shirt and tie was one of the supervisors.

Community Kitchen Was Used by Workers' Families

Shown at right is one of the community kitchens provided for workers' families by Balfour-Guthrie. One can imagine the stir caused when a group of women were cooking side-by-side. The women were generally good-humored and learned how to cooperate with each other to ease the problems inherent in this situation.

The only time Balfour-Guthrie was faced with labor unrest was during the early depression years, when there were too many workers for too few jobs and the company offered wages that were much too low. John Miller, newly elected sheriff, eased the problem by persuading the company to pay higher wages and the workers to bring their problems to his attention before going on strike.

Downtown Brentwood in the Late 1940s

By the1940s Balfour-Guthrie had sold much of its land to individual farmers, in 15-acre and 20-acre parcels. Some smaller parcels were sold as home sites. Thus Brentwood quit being a "company town" and became a delightful small city. The picture above, taken in the late 1940s, will look familiar even to newcomers because the same buildings are still there (but with different occupants). The Bank of America at left started as the Bank of Brentwood in 1913, then became the Bank of Antioch before becoming part of A.P. Giannini's great chain. (Now the building is not a bank at all.) Across the street was the variety store, the Delta Theatre, and several other businesses. As can be seen, diagonal parking provided room for a lot more cars than the present system.

The Fabulous
Byron Times

A most notable citizen of Byron was Harry Hammond, who came in 1906 to publish the weekly *Byron Times*. He also published a bi-annual series of 15 magazine-style special editions, printed on slick paper, with full-color covers and many illustrations. Mr. Hammond promoted Contra Costa County to the world, sending copies to influential people everywhere. Old copies of these beautiful special editions now command high prices at antique booksellers. Mr. Hammond was honored in his later years by Governor James Rolph, Jr., who appointed him to the post of State Printer.

Byron Grew Up Around S.P. Depot

The San Pablo & Tulare Railroad (later merged with Southern Pacific) completed a line from Los Banos to Martinez in 1878. The railroad built a depot about five miles southeast of Brentwood and named it Byron. This was the beginning of the town. The first building was a hotel put up by F. Wilkening in 1878. Within a few years there were three saloons, two blacksmith shops, a general store, a harness shop, a livery stable, and a post office—with a population of 60, mostly the town business people, who served farmers of the region.

Early settlers in the Byron/Point of Timber community included George Fellows, E.D. Grigsby, C.J. Preston, and A.T. and Volney Taylor. For a time Byron was a lively shipping point between Stockton and San Francisco and the population grew considerably. Produce from Point of Timber and Eden Plain was shipped via the S.P. depot at Byron.

The photo shows the main business street of Byron in 1917. Several farmers had parked their Model Ts to drop into the farm implement store in the foreground or the saloon just down the street. A dog is crossing the street after waiting for a car to go by. Byron merchants proudly hung a sign over the street to proclaim the town's identity.

As trucking firms phased out the railroad and the nearby hot springs fell into disuse, the town's business dwindled away. But Byron is a town that has refused to die. Its Main Street now boasts a restaurant, beauty salon, bar, post office, mini-mart/gas station, and offices of the irrigation district. And if you live in nearby Discovery Bay, your mail address is Byron.

Byron Hot Springs Attracted Celebrities; Later Became a Prison

The curative powers of the mineral springs in the low foothills east of Mount Diablo were first discovered by Indians hundreds of years ago. In the early 1850s American and Mexican travelers bathed in the springs to obtain relief from rheumatism and other ailments. Eventually these visitors built a bath house and a pit for mud baths. In 1863 Lewis Risdon Mead came to California to assist his uncle, John O. Risdon, who had filed a claim on the land around the springs. The U.S. issued a land patent and Lewis Mead was placed in charge of developing Byron Hot Springs.

The hotel, guest cottages, and bath houses he built are shown in the 1892 drawing at right. The main hotel building was next to the flag pole. The spa became a popular vacation resort for wealthy tourists from all over the U.S. and Europe. The hotel burned down in 1901. Mead immediately built a larger Spanish-Moorish style hotel on the site, shown in the photo below. It opened in 1902. A horse-drawn stage coach met the guests who arrived at the little town of Byron, 2-1/2 miles away. Many guests also came by automobile over roads that had been built to the spa.

There were some 50 springs, varying in mineral content and ranging from hot to cold. They contained sulphur, sodium, potassium, calcium, and other minerals. Mineral water was pumped to the hotel for individual baths. Separate buildings housed the mud baths, sulphur baths, and a swimming pool. In 1912 this second hotel was destroyed by fire. Mead built a third hotel--a four-story fireproof brick and concrete building.

In the 1920s this hotel was a gathering place for famous movie stars and other celebrities, who came to soak in the hot mud and mineral waters. However interest waned in Byron Hot Springs and its era ended in the 1930s Depression years. During World War II the hotel was taken over by the War Department to house high-ranking German, Japanese, and Italian prisoners.

After the war the former resort was taken over by the Greek Orthodox Church as a retreat and a retirement home for elderly priests.

After the church discontinued using the property a series of promoters each tried to revive the place as a resort or for residential development, thus far to no avail.

Southern Pacific built this little Mission-Revival style station at the hot springs in the early 1900s.

Sailing Vessels Hauled Grain from Babbe's Landing

Frederick Babbe came to California from Prussia in 1850, worked in the gold mines for a year, returned to Europe briefly, and then came back to California to settle at a site near the San Joaquin River in eastern Contra Costa. This place became known as Babbe's Landing. Mr. Babbe spent some $30,000 reclaiming the lands, building levees 5 to 7 feet high and 20 to 30 feet at the base. A 42-foot wide canal was dug from the river, permitting the passage of 100-ton sailing vessels to the landing, where they were loaded with grain and produce for the San Francisco market. Some 3,000 to 4,000 tons a year were being shipped. The photo shows a load of baled hay on a schooner-rigged scow about to leave Babbe's Landing circa 1912.

Knightsen: Away From the Hubbub

Knightsen was the name of a Santa Fe depot established near Eden Plain in 1898. Dairy farms were already operating in this area and had been shipping their milk and cream via Southern Pacific. With the new depot being more convenient, Santa Fe got most of the dairy shipments. Celery and asparagus were also grown near Knightsen. Most of these crops were shipped from nearby Babbe's Landing until the mid-1920s, when trucking companies got most of the shipments. Knightsen has continued over the years as a small country village, with a few dozen homes, a park, school, post office, and a couple of stores. The photo shows Delta Road about 1912. The homes belonged to Bob Clark, Sam Redmond, Bill Redmond, and a Mrs. Heidorn.

Oakley's Wild Past: Gambling Parlors, Opium Dens, Crooked Bankers, Prostitutes--All In or Near the Notorious Oakley Hotel

A hundred years ago the site of Oakley consisted of sand dunes covered with chaparral and wild flowers and populated mostly by jackrabbits, coyotes, quail, and wild pigeons. James O'Hara, a settler from Maine, bought some of this land from the government for $5 an acre in 1887. He cleared 80 acres and planted an almond orchard. Later he planted 160 acres more in nut and fruit trees. Continuing to expand, he eventually owned 700 acres under cultivation. He was the first of many orchardists in the area.

The Santa Fe Railroad started rolling through the orchards in 1900, providing an incentive for R.C. Marsh to start the town of Oakley. Several merchants started stores in the new town: Frank Silva, Jerry O'Meara, Joseph Jesse, Henry Jannassee, and Arnold Van Kathoven. A blacksmith shop was started by John Augusto and a lumber yard was started by his brother Joseph.

Mr. and Mrs. S. Dal Porto came to town in 1908 from Jackson, California. They built the Oakley Hotel and a town hall. In the next few years A. G. Ramos opened a harness shop, M. A. Ferrell started a general store, and—in the '20s—a public library opened.

The principal business of the town was packing and shipping local produce: celery and asparagus from the Delta and grapes and almonds from the Oakley area. There were many packing sheds lined up along the railroad tracks.

The population was cosmopolitan: Chinese worked in the fields; men from India worked on the dikes and levees in the Delta; Mexicans worked in the packing sheds, and there were farmers and merchants of Irish, Portuguese, German, and Italian descent, to name a few.

There were many more men than women; prostitutes prospered in the upstairs rooms of the Oakley Hotel. Downstairs there were Chinese men smoking opium. Several of the stores on Ruby Street were gambling joints, where stacks of $20 gold pieces changed hands from minute to minute.

Like many other towns of its type, Oakley was a wild place in the first decades of this century. In the late 1920s a new scandal broke which cost a lot of people their savings. The cashier of the Bank of Oakley and his accomplice, the Santa Fe agent, were speculating on the stock market with the bank's money. When the market crashed in November 1929 the bank couldn't cover the losses and closed.

Oakley has changed. The packing sheds disappeared after World War II when refrigerated trucks started picking up crated vegetables in the fields. The gambling joints, opium dens, and prostitutes are mostly gone and subdivisions have been eating away at the orchards and vineyards for some time now. The old Oakley Hotel building stills stands, as do several other early buildings along Highway 4. An endless stream of cars goes down the highway, but most of the drivers are new people, who know little about Oakley's past and see only a quiet country town.

Country Charm: Iron House School Served Farm Children

The Iron House School District was formed in 1896 to start a school for farmers' children in the area between Oakley and Knightsen. Silas and Carlos Emerson sold a square-acre school site to the district for $100, with the proviso that the property would revert to the Emersons when and if it were no longer used for a school. The *Iron House* name came from a nearby corrugated-iron storage building called the Iron House. The school was built by Sprague & Scott of Brentwood, who were also responsible for its unique design. The lumber was purchased from the Beede lumberyard in Antioch, shipped up the river and along Dutch Slough to Babbe's Landing, and thence hauled to the building site. The school bell came from a foundry in San Francisco. The photo shows the school in 1907. The group of children on the left are Enos Mattos, Roland Silvera, Manuel Cabral, Frank Nugent, Manuel Silva, and Albert Jesse. In the center are Winnie Cabral, Mae Miller, Celia Jesse,

an unidentified girl, Agnes Cabral, Frances Miller, Henrietta Terra, Minnie Miller, Kiko Jujita, Annie Miller, Bill Vengely, and Madeline Vengely. On the right are Lucy Silva, Frances Bagwell, Lizette O'Meara, and Annie Silvera. Small school districts like Iron House had a tough time making ends meet in the 1930s Depression era. The district was virtually forced to close the school in 1935. The students were bused—over the protests of their parents—to a school in Oakley, and the Emerson family got the property back, as per the deed. The schoolhouse was converted to a home. In 1972 the Emerson family had it moved from its original location, at the corner of Sellers Avenue and Cypress Road, to another spot about a quarter-mile back from Cypress Road. Fisher House Movers of Stockton did the job using two Caterpillar tractors and a big Kenworthy truck. One of the former students at Iron House was Antioch banker Victor Parachini.

Officers Seized Moonshine Still

The Volstead Act created jobs for law enforcement people, who were kept busy all during the Prohibition Era looking for and sometimes finding sellers and users of alcoholic beverages. Drugs other than alcohol were not much of a problem during this period; cocaine, marijuana, and morphine were legal in the 1920s, and therefore not profitable for sellers and largely ignored by the public. Various Contra Costa newspapers had frequent accounts of arrests relating to alcohol. One such arrest was made on Thursday, July 5, 1923, when a trio of officers seized a moonshine still hidden in a barn on a ranch in the Sand Mound section near Bethel Island. Several gallons of illicit liquor were also taken. The officers posed for this photo with their trophy, displayed on the bed of a truck. Left to right are Martinez Constable B.B. Rogers, Concord Constable John Ott, and Deputy Sheriff E.A. Call. Three suspects had been arrested: Jack Forble, Louis Zanotta, and Carlo Grasso.

San Pablo Started as a Little Village in the 1820s; Later Gained Fame for Annual Festival

Years before California became a state a little Mexican village began in the 1820s on part of Don Francisco Castro's land grant. That village was called San Pablo. In the early 1850s a road was completed between Oakland and Martinez, with San Pablo being the place where horses were changed, allowing passengers to get food and drink at the San Pablo Hotel or one of the 18 saloons in the town. Many Portuguese sailors who had originally visited San Pablo in whaling boats came back in the 1850s to buy farms. The former sailors and their families brought a 600-year-old tradition with them from the old country--the Holy Ghost Festival. The festival has been held annually in San Pablo for more than 130 years. Some of the events include the crowning of a queen by the parish priest, a dance at the church hall, and a parade from the church. There is also a feast featuring *soupa*, a special seasoned gravy eaten with French bread. The photo below shows the queen and her attendants in the early 1950s. The festival has attracted huge crowds every year, including many who are not members of the lodge which sponsors it.

In 1872 San Pablo had an American flag made to order, measuring 15 feet by 22 feet, which was hoisted up an 80-foot flagpole on July 4th that year. It was then the largest flag in the state. It was raised on important holidays up until 1898, when the flagpole had began to rot and the flag had shown some signs of wear. Since then the flag has been taken out of its vault and displayed on a protected wall on patriotic holidays.

Chapter 13

The San Pablo School, shown above, was built in 1900 on Market Street. Its first student body consisted of 150 children who had come from three smaller schools which had been closed to be replaced by this larger new school. Walter T. Helms, fresh out of college, got his first job here as principal and teacher. He later became superintendent of the Richmond School District. After his retirement in 1949 he helped found the Contra Costa County Historical Society and served many years as its treasurer.

The San Pablo Fire Department started in 1926 with 25 unpaid volunteers. In 1928 the department accquired a fire engine, which was kept at M.G. Moitoza's auto repair shop. "Mose" Moitoza called the volunteers into action by sounding a siren on top of the garage. In 1938 the town built its first fire station. When the town was incorporated in 1948 the fire department achieved full professional status.

This was the largest flag in California in 1872. It originally had 35 stars; two stars were added when two more states joined the union. The man in this 1953 photo is Fritz Carlfield, keeper of the flag.

Before Richmond It Was Ellis Landing

Ellis Landing was the beginning of the Port of Richmond, 41 years before the city was founded. George Ellis, a '49er who didn't strike it rich in the gold diggings, turned to the shipping business. In 1859 he built his wharf in the mudflats near an Indian shellmound. With two flat-bottomed sailboats (that he could sail only at high tide) he ferried passengers and farm produce to San Francisco. The painting reproduced above shows his home, warehouses, and one of the sailboats at dock. The boy fishing in the foreground may have been John Nystrom, who grew up be manager of Ellis Landing.

Bernardo Fernandez Shipped Grain From Pinole Landing

Bernardo Fernandez, one of the founders of Pinole, was a Portuguese sailor who had seen the world, and then picked a beautiful spot on San Pablo Bay to settle down. In 1854 he purchased a schooner and started a water freight business between Pinole and San Francisco. Shipping grain became his main business. He prospered over the years. At the time the drawing at left was made, in 1878, he owned four large warehouses for storing grain, three schooners, a long wharf, a three-gabled house, a lovely hillside orchard, a general store (next to the house) and other real estate in and around the village of Pinole. Cars went on tracks from his warehouse to and right on the wharf, drawn by horses. There was a railroad depot on his land, shown in the drawing just to the right of the wharf. The combination passenger-freight train puffing along the shore was enroute from Oakland to Valona.

Fernandez Mansion Became a Boarding House for Beatniks

After Bernardo Fernandez's first house burned down he built a new one a little way up the hill from the Southern Pacific station. It was a mansion, one of the most beautiful homes in California--a fine example of Classic Mannerist Italianate style. The Fernandez family lived in the mansion for many years, even after the death of the grain magnate in 1912. After the family sold the mansion it had a succession of owners. The photo shows how it looked in 1956 in the midst of tree-shaded grounds. Later in the 1950s it became a boarding house for self-styled "beatniks," whose eccentric lifestyle caused damage to the property over and above the wear and tear wrought by time. In 1970 the dilapidated old home was purchased by Dr. Joseph Mariotti, president of the Pinole Historical Society. He had the mansion repaired and restored to its original magnificence. It is considered to be one of the important historical landmarks of Contra Costa County.

Downtown Pinole in 1915

In its early years Pinole consisted of a half-dozen houses, thirteen saloons, a post office, and the Fernandez general store. The most notable people in town were Dutch Henry, an old German butcher; Riley, the Chinese fruit and vegetable man; John Henry, the town hermit (who ran one of the 13 saloons and who was thought to have buried $5,000 in gold coins in back of the saloon, which is not known to have been found). There were also a few more conventional folk, such as E.M. Downer, who came to Pinole as the Southern Pacific station agent and ended up starting the Bank of Pinole. He later became president of the Richmond-based multi-branch Mechanics Bank. The photo shows downtown Pinole about 1915. You're looking down Main Street, which was dominated by telephone poles on one side and power poles on the other. A few pedestrians and a horse and wagon can be seen outdoors. The Pinole Hotel is just down the street. There are two saloons in the foreground at left and another at right, with a customer looking out from the doorway.

159

Chinese Had the Worst Jobs At Hercules Powder Company

California Powder Works, makers of dynamite and blasting powder, moved in 1879 to a then-isolated spot on the shore of San Pablo Bay, an appropriate place for a plant liable to have accidental explosions. The plant was constructed and into production in two years.

Next to the new plant the company built a town for its employees, segregated by a caste system: The superintendent lived in a mansion; the managers lived on "The Hill;" the white laborers lived in "The Village," and the Chinese laborers lived in two long barracks buildings.

The Chinese, who constituted the majority of the work force, were the lowest paid (12-1/2 cents an hour) and had the most dangerous jobs -- in the nitroglycerine lines. From 1881 to 1919 59 workers were killed by explosions, most of them Chinese.

In 1900, wanting to make their own laws, company officials incorporated the site of the plant and company town as the City of Hercules, named after the company's potent product, Hercules black powder. With a population of 100 it was the smallest incorporated city in California.

In 1906 E.I. DuPont de Nemours Powder Company took over the California Powder Works, but in 1912, moving to comply with a federal court order, the California firm was separated from DuPont and reorganized as the Hercules Powder Company. Since the stockholders of DuPont and the stockholders of Hercules were the same people, there was no real change.

A 13-foot-tall semi-nude statue of the mythological Greek hero Hercules was placed on a hill near the plant in 1913. There was a series of complaints about the nudity from some passers-by, presumably not art connoiseurs, and the statue was destroyed (by dynamite, what else?) in the late 1920s.

The company made munitions for two world wars as well as blasting powder for peacetime uses such as highway construction.

Despite safety precautions, disastrous explosions occured in 1944, 1948, and 1953, leaving many dead and injured. With homes crowding in around the city of Hercules, a concern for

CHINESE WORKERS AT HERCULES, ABOUT 1900

safety led the company to quit making explosives. In 1964 the plant was converted to the manufacture of fertilizers. This, however, caused a lot of air and water pollution. Measures to eliminate the problem cost the company millions of dollars. In 1976 the plant was sold to Valley Nitrogen producers, a fertilizer company that owned other plants in California. After a strike in 1977 the plant was shut down. The land around the plant, which had been a buffer zone, was sold to developers, who built huge tracts of homes for Bay Area commuters. The population zoomed from 100 to 10,000 in ten years.

The first traffic signal and the first pizza parlor came to Hercules in 1983, but that is the beginning of another story.

HERCULES POWDER COMPANY PLANT ON SAN PABLO BAY, ABOUT 1918.

THE GREEK HERO HERCULES

Selby Smelter Produced Gold, Silver, Lead, Zinc, and a Lot of Pollution

Once the pride of West County, the Selby smelter operated for 85 years--until 1970--when it was found to be more of a hazard than an asset. Its four huge blast furnaces ran day and night, separating metals from their ores. Thousands of tons of metals--lead, zinc, gold, and silver--were shipped from the Selby docks (shown below) all over the world. The firm had been started in San Francisco by Thomas Selby in 1850. In 1883 Selby decided to move his smelter and refinery to a spot on San Pablo Bay, at the northwest corner of Contra Costa County, which he named after himself. It took two years to get the new plant going. A crew of 60 men did the initial excavating and grading, and then the buildings shown in the upper photo were constructed. In 1885, the first year of operation, the plant was producing $30,000 worth of gold and 30,000 ounces of silver each day. These metals were shipped to the U.S. Mint in San Francisco. The Selby plant had its own well, 620 feet deep. It was using 400 tons of coal per month from the mines at Nortonville and Somersville. Many of the 600 employees of the smelter lived in company-owned houses in the nearby village of Tormey (named after Patrick Tormey, who once owned the land). The site of Tormey, incidentally, was where the men of the deAnza expedition were entertained and given gifts by friendly Indians in 1776. The Selby smelter was sold

to American Smelting and Refining Company, a gigantic international corporation, in 1886. Lead and zinc smelting became the principal business at Selby. Also at this location was a cartridge factory, using a machine-operated shell loader invented by George Standish, the plow manufacturer from Pacheco. In 1907 a shot tower was built. Molten lead was dropped from the top of the tower and turned into little pellets on the way down. These photos were taken about 1910. The upper photo shows the shot tower at left and the landmark smokestack at right. A rail siding is in the foreground. In the lower photo a three-masted freighter is tied up at the Selby wharf, having just unloaded the huge pile of coke in the foreground. In 1953 a zinc fuming plant (for producing zinc oxide) was constructed at a cost of $4 million. Selby was busier than ever and a lot of money was being made by American Smelting, but all was not well. It was discovered that a slag heap on the land had been leaching poisonous lead and arsenic into San Pablo Bay for some 85 years and, furthermore, that workers breathing the fumes at the plant were getting sick. The plant was closed in 1970. The next 17 years were spent in arguments over who was going to clean up the mess: American Smelting, the actual polluter; the state, which owned the land and had leased it to American Smelting, or Wickland Oil, which wanted to build a refinery on the site. Finally, in 1987, it was decided to split the $9 million cleanup cost among the parties, with the state picking up a large share and the taxpayers getting a raw deal, as usual.

Refinery of the Union Oil Company at Oleum
—from *Contra Costa News,* Martinez, 1887

Rodeo Was a Cattlemen's Town, and Then an Oilmen's Town

Rodeo got its name from the rodeos held there in the days when raising cattle was the major industry in Contra Costa. The town was established in 1890 by Patrick Tormey, who owned a nearby meat-packing plant. The town grew rapidly. By 1893 it had its own daily newspaper. In 1895 Union Oil purchased a large tract of land in Rodeo and called it Oleum.

This was site of the first refinery in Contra Costa, pictured above as it looked in 1897, with its railroad siding and wharves. Many of the refinery workers have lived in Rodeo. One of the town's old landmarks, the Rio Theatre, was the subject of heated controversy when it was converted to a rock-concert hall in the late 1970s.

RICHARD STEGE

ANOTHER INDUSTRY:
Frog Legs for San Francisco Restaurants

In 1870 an Oakland furniture store owner, Richard Stege, married a rich widow, Mrs. C.C. Quilfeldt, who had been operating a 600-acre ranch. Mr. Stege closed his store and took over the ranch. He turned it into a showplace, with magnificent gardens and four ponds, in which he raised frogs to provide frog legs for elegant restaurants in San Francisco. The little town of Stege (later part of Richmond) started on this ranch. Several factories moved to Stege at the turn of the century, as noted elsewhere in this book. Richard Stege's gardens and ponds eventually became East Shore Park.

East Brother Lighthouse in San Pablo Bay

East Brother Light Station was built on a rocky one-acre island in San Pablo Bay. Its light has guided sailors through fog and darkness continuously since 1874. The light station consists of three Victorian buildings. It was one of the second group of light stations to be built along the west coast. Of the 17 lighthouses in and around San Francisco Bay, East Brother is the oldest one still in operation. It has seen the passage of clipper ships and the closing of the nation's last whaling station at nearby Point San Pablo. From 1874 to 1969 the station was manned by keepers and their families and by rotating crews of the U.S. Coast Guard. And then the light and foghorn were automated; it was no longer necessary for a lighthouse keeper to live on the island. The buildings were boarded up for 10 years, with only maintenance visits by the Coast Guard. In 1979 a nonprofit organization was formed to restore the station and operate it as a small hotel and a living museum of maritime history. The station is now open to visitors, who can take a tour of the facility, enjoy the great views, breathe some exhilerating salt-flavored air, hobnob with seagulls, have an elegant old fashioned dinner there, stay overnight, and have breakfast the next morning before leaving.

Mr. Macdonald Made a Deal with Santa Fe -- and Founded Richmond

Real estate man A.S. Macdonald came out to the old Castro grant near the bay in 1895 on a duck hunt, but the ducks were flying to high to hit. He decided to quit and go for a walk. Looking over the bay from the top of Potrero Hill, he conceived an idea for a transcontinental rail terminal and port. Passengers, freight, and even entire cars could be ferried across to San Francisco, saving many miles. Mr. Macdonald promoted his deal and the Santa Fe established its western terminus here. Mr. Macdonald then purchased ranch land from George Barrett, subdived it into 5,000 business and residential lots, and the town of Richmond was born.

On July 3, 1900, after several years of track laying, tunnel construction, and building of ferry slips, the Santa Fe ferried 200 passengers from San Francisco to Point Richmond, where they boarded the railroad's first through train to Chicago, with public officials and a huge crowd to see them off. It was a great beginning for Santa Fe and for Richmond.

Richmond was mostly a tent town in the summer of 1900. The first train station was a box car on stilts. The first grocery store and newspaper office had been established by Lyman Naugle at the foot of Barrett Street, but the town's first growth was along Washington Avenue. The town grew rapidly to meet housing, schooling, and other needs of people coming to work for Santa Fe and other firms. Santa Fe moved its shops from Stockton to Richmond in January 1901, thus becoming the first major employer in the new town. The rail yards encompassed many acres by 1915 when the photo at right was taken.

A.S. Macdonald
Founder of Richmond

Left: Horse and buggy days on Macdonald Avenue, the main business street in Richmond, named for the town founder. They weren't dreaming of red and green traffic lights when this picture was taken in 1912. Note the fashions of the two women in the foreground.

Early-Day Industries
Got a Town on the Move

By the turn of the century, Stauffer Chemical, California Cap Works, and Metropolitan Match Factory had located in Stege (later part of Richmond). Then, with the advent of the Santa Fe, industrial development boomed and Richmond was visualized as the American Liverpool.

The biggest industry came early. From a Southern Pacific train one day in October 1901 stepped W.S. Rheem and two other Standard Oil officials. They drove a horse and buggy to a tract the company had purchased just north of town. Before sundown Rheem had hired men to clear the land -- and within eight months the largest refinery on the Pacific Coast was in operation. In 1902 the refinery produced 10,000 barrels of petroleum products. By the 1950s the refinery was processing 140,000 barrels of oil daily and making a huge variety of products, including gasoline and motor oil, wax for milk cartons, shoe polish, floor polish, bread wrappers, lipstick, paint, printers' ink, and more.

In 1907 a ship canal had been built to spur commercial development and the roster of industries included California Wineries Association, Richmond Machine and Iron Works, Berkeley Steel, Richmond Manufacturing, Richmond Pottery, and two brick factories.

The Pullman Shops came in 1910, employing 450 people -- including blacksmiths, tin smiths, plumbers, electricians, seamstresses, upholsterers, mechanics, dyers, cleaners, and locksmiths --to repair and refurbish their elegant sleeping cars, which were leased to all major railroads.

Other early industries were American Radiator and Standard Sanitary, Certain-teed Products, and Princeton Knitting Mills. The latter firm employed mostly women, who sat at rows and rows of sewing machines and knitting machines.

STANDARD OIL REFINERY, ABOUT 1916

CALIFORNIA WINERIES ASSOCIATION—"WINEHAVEN," about 1910

INTERIOR OF PULLMAN SHOPS, ABOUT 1916

They Jumped Out of Bed at the Clang of a Bell

Richmond had an unpaid volunteer fire department for 20 years. There were five volunteer companies, composed of men who at the clang of a bell left their businesses in the daytime -- or jumped out of bed at any hour of the night -- to fight the community's great enemy. The volunteer force began with Richmond Volunteer Fire Company No. 1, which was organized at a town meeting held on Wednesday, June 12, 1901, at the Critchett Hotel in Point Richmond. Two disastrous fires had already ravaged the town, and then, the day after the 19-member fire company was formed it had a major fire to fight, which started in the storehouse of the railroad shops. A switch engine was brought to the scene with a supply of water which doused the flames just before they reached 6,000 gallons of oil that had been stored in the building. The nostalgic photo above was taken on July 4, 1909, and shows three men of the original company with the original hose cart and bell. The men are (left to right) William Ellis, sub-chief; R.L. Adams, fireman, and John Murray, chief. The baby sitting in the hose cart is Lillian Vance, step-niece of Mr. Ellis. Copies of this picture were given as souvenirs to guests at the fire company's semi-annual banquet at Fraternal Hall on Saturday evening, January 29, 1910. The program included whist, dancing, and musical and literary selections, with the food being served at the late hour of 11 p.m. Parties like these often lasted all night in those times. The banquet was typical of the fund-raising events put on by the various fire companies to get money for equipment, hoses, etc.

'APPY 'ARRY MAGINNIS

ROUND 6

KOSHER MARTIN THE WINNER

MIDGET CHARLEY GEER

SHERIFF VEALE CAME IN LATE

Boxing Matches Drew Big Crowds

One of America's most famous cartoonists Thomas A. Dorgan ("Tad") of the *San Francisco Bulletin* came to Richmond on June 20, 1902, to record his impressions of a prize fight between Eddie Martin and Jack McGinnis, held at Curry's Opera House. Some of his work is shown above, including a delightful caricature of Contra Costa Sheriff R.R. Veale. There was a huge crowd at the fight, which included well-known sports figures Jim Murphy, Martin Murphy, Jerry Cope, Arizona Charley, Joe Moitoza, and Henry Berzone. Martin won the fight with a knock-out in the 6th round. Professional and amateur boxing matches were a popular form of entertainment for many years, with frequent fights featuring local men, and occasional matches between highly rated professionals. A 45-round world championship fight took place in Richmond on February 22, 1910. Lightweight champion Battling Nelson defended his title against Ad Wolgast. A 20,000-seat arena was built for the fight. Spectators came from all over on special trains and ferryboats. It rained the day of the fight, but 10,000 die-hard fans came anyhow. Just as the fight started the rain stopped. Nelson was so battered in the 40th round that the referee stopped the fight and Wolgast was proclaimed the new champion.

A YEAR BEFORE THE WRIGHT BROTHERS:

But the Flying Machine Never Flew

The unusual craft shown flying over Point Richmond in 1902 was the invention of Professor Robert H. Botts—but the picture was a composite, combining a photo of a small model of the flying machine with the photo of the scene—in other words, a fake. It was part of the advertising used by the inventor to raise capital to manuafacture his invention.

Professor Botts had arrived in Point Richmond sometime during the winter of 1900-01. He announced that he held patents on a new steam engine and steam-powered flying machine. His experiments had been written up in the *Scientific American,* which referred to him as a mechanical genius. He displayed the model of his airship in San Francisco and Richmond. There were two horizontal propellers to provide lift and there was also a vertical driving propeller at the stern.

In February 1902 Professor Botts announced plans for an aerial expedition to the North Pole, composed of scientists traveling in two of his patented airships. Each ship was to be equipped with motion picture cameras and the Marconi system of communication (i.e., radio). The next month he began selling shares in the World's Aerial Navigation Company. Enough money was raised to build the first airship in a workshop atop Nichol Nob.

A crowd gathered at Nichol Nob on the day of the test flight. All was in readiness. And then a sudden windstorm blew the craft down the steep slopes, dashing it to pieces—and dashing the hopes of the professor. He left town, apparently broken-hearted. And the next year, at Kitty Hawk, North Carolina, the Wright Brothers were the ones who made history.

Richmond Streetcar Motormen Used to Stop and Shoot Rabbits

Richmond streetcars, like the one shown above, were a popular form of transportation in old times. In the year 1910, for example, the streetcar line carried 2.7 million passengers!

The photographer snapped a conductor and two motormen posing for posterity while two passengers waited patiently for the car to get moving. (For our younger readers, a motorman was the guy who ran the streetcar; a conductor collected fares.)

A conductor generally wore a change-maker on his waist, like the one in the picture. This was a gadget that accepted coins through various slots and released needed change by pushing levers.

Note that there were open-air sections on each end of the streetcar; these were the smoking sections. A lot of people liked to ride in these sections because they could see more -- and it was easier to get on and off the car.

The East Shore and Suburban Railway had been organized in 1904 and merged with Oakland Traction Company in 1911. At that time the company had 17 miles of track in Richmond plus tracks to the county line and branch lines to San Pablo and Grand Canyon Park.

The Richmond line ran along Ohio Street, then on Sixth Street to Macdonald Avenue, and thence to San Pablo Avenue. When the service first started Ohio Street and Macdonald Avenue were yet to be paved. Passengers were likely to step into a sea of mud when alighting from a streetcar on these streets. Ohio Street was open country. Sometimes a motorman would stop his car and take a shot at a jack rabbit or two.

Port of Richmond Grew To Greatness under Fred D. Parr

Even before Richmond was a town -- or had a name -- it was a port. Water commerce started in the 1820s, when New England ship captains anchored off shore to trade for hides and tallow with the rancheros; however, Captain Ellis was the pioneer who actually built a wharf and a warehouse in 1859.

The natural harbor attracted Santa Fe and Standard Oil at the turn of the century. From that time through the 1920s immense steamship wharves and warehouses were built, channels dredged, and a retaining wall constructed. These projects, costing millions of dollars, were financed by private capital, city bond issues, and federal grants. E.J. Garrard, Congressman Charles F. Curry, Henry A. Johnston, and other public-spirited citizens provided the vision and leadership.

Richmond's next step toward its destiny was a partnership agreement signed in 1926 between the City and Fred D. Parr to operate the harbor. Mr. Parr had already founded a steamship line and managed the Port of Oakland. He planned and directed vast further harbor improvements, secured better rail facilities, and induced giant industrial firms to locate on the waterfront. First of these was Ford, which -- with a $10,000-a-day payroll -- helped Richmond's fortunes for a quarter century. In the ensuing years more than 100 major manufacturing and distributing companies have located here and Richmond has become the greatest port on the Pacific Coast.

The photo shows one of several wharves of the Parr-Richmond Terminal Company. A combination cargo and passenger ship is at dock, with a crowd gathered for an informal bon voyage party.

But What Happened to the Indian?

The City of Richmond really began along Washington Avenue in Point Richmond—the neighborhood depicted above. Washington Avenue had a streetcar line running down its middle at the time this photo was taken, around 1920.

Futter's store sold Can't Bust 'Em jeans and other clothing, along with a line of dry goods. The sign boasted "Honest Values—Our Hobby: Pleased Customers." This was a time when both automobiles and horse-drawn vehicles traveled the streets. The automobiles often broke down, which prompted little boys to yell "Get a horse!" at unfortunate motorists. The street on the right is Park Place. This area has been called The Triangle by several generations of Point Richmond people.

The statue in front of Futter's, which is a little hard to see clearly in this photo, was of an Indian. It was placed there

in 1909 by the West Side Improvement Club at a cost of $1,500. The bronze Indian was a cherished landmark for years until one day in 1942 when he was toppled by a brisk windstorm and broken to bits.

Just around the corner from Futter's was The Baltic, at 135 Park Place, the first tavern in Point Richmond—started in 1904. Its backbar and mirror were brought over from San Francisco just before the 1906 earthquake. The Baltic has always been a saloon; it was a speakeasy during Prohibition.

Through the years parts of the Baltic building have served at various times as city hall, residential apartments, funeral parlour, and bordello. One of its walls was for a time the fourth wall of Richmond's first firehouse and police station. Jack London mentioned The Baltic in his writings. In later years it has become a restaurant, serving Italian cuisine.

Ford Assembly Plant Produced a Million Cars in Richmond

One of the first giant industrial firms to locate on the Richmond waterfront was the Ford Motor Company. With a $10,000 per day payroll Ford helped the city's fortunes for a quarter of a century. The Ford assembly plant opened in 1931. The dedication program featured a speech by U.S. Senator Samuel Shortridge. Some 20,000 people attended the ceremonies. After the senator's speech the audience waited expectantly as J.J. Tynan, a Bethlehem Steel executive, rose to pull the cord of the factory whistle. This was to be the signal to start the factory. He pulled the

cord. Nothing happened. He yanked harder. Still no sound. Then a quick-witted young man ran out to the docks, boarded a ship, sounded its whistle, and thus started the assembly line. The plant employed 1,650 workers, who assembled about 50,000 cars and trucks a year. Thirty carloads of parts were shipped into the plant each day. The finished vehicles were sold by 500 Ford dealers in the West. During World War II the Ford plant made jeeps for the army. (Incidentally, "jeep" was the generic nickname of those cars long before it became a so-called trademark.) The photo above shows Dave Rose, Sheriff R.R. Veale, and plant manager Clarence Bullwinkle witnessing completion of the first car. The photo at left shows workers lowering a body onto a chassis on the assembly line in 1949. By the early 1950s it became apparent that the plant was too small. There wasn't room to expand on the crowded waterfront, and so the assembling of Ford trucks and cars moved to a new plant a mile north of San Jose.

The 1940s:
A Wartime City of Shipbuilders

President Franklin Delano Roosevelt issued the call to arms in 1940: our country was to become the arsenal of democracy. Soon it became evident that on our ability to do this rested the destiny of the free world.

England contracted with the newly organized Todd-California Company in Richmond for 30 ships to replace those lost in German U-boat attacks. Contracts from Washington, D.C., followed. Suddenly the small city of 23,000 became a perpetual city of lights as one, two, three, and then four shipyards operated around the clock.

Population zoomed to 123,000 by 1942. Transportation, housing, feeding, care of small children, education, medical care, recreation — these became great concerns of federal and local government. Shuttle trains were operated, gigantic housing projects were built, nurseries were established, new schools, classroom additions, clinics, and community centers were built. And yet, during most of the war years off-duty shift workers jammed the streets in nocturnal revel, new arrivals slept in their cars or in city parks, and stores were usually "sold out" of meat, sugar, and nylons.

Up to the middle of 1944 the Richmond yards had produced 563 Liberty ships, more than had been produced in any other place in the country. These ships, vital to the Allied war effort, were dubbed "Ugly Ducklings" by the sailors who served aboard them. Victory ships, LSTs, troop transports, and other vessels were also built in Richmond. Through unique assemblyline methods and the ingenuity of shipyard men and women Richmond set the pace for the entire nation in production—making and breaking many records. In recognition, local shipyards received many "E" (for Efficiency) flags.

THE BIG THREE

Here are three men who made history in the shipbuilding industry in Richmond: (Left to right) Henry J. Kaiser, leader of vast war industrial enterprises (and the founder of a health plan that bears his name); Fred D. Parr, outstanding figure in ship terminal and other industrial activities (and the founder of Goodwill Industries), and S. D. Bechtel, affiliated with the fabulous Six Companies. This picture was taken at a Chamber of Commerce luncheon to commemorate the breaking of ground for Shipyard One in 1940.

After a brief ceremony another ship goes down the ways. This was an almost daily occurence in Richmond during World War 2

The Last Days of the Ferry to San Rafael

People came from all sides of the Bay to take farewell trips on the beloved boats in August 1956—the busiest time in the history of the ferry service

The last days of the Richmond-San Rafael ferryboats are depicted in this poignant photograph, taken in mid-1956. Two off-duty boats are shown in the foreground. A third ferryboat is steaming across the bay, heading for the slip shown in the middle of the photo. There are about a dozen cars lined up on the long wharf waiting to board the boat when it arrives.

Richmond-San Rafael ferry service started in 1915, the same year as the wonderful Panama-Pacific International Exposition in San Francisco. The ferries stopped running on August 31, 1956--and the new sway-backed bridge, shown in the background, opened to traffic the next day.

The last two weeks of August were the busiest weeks in the 41-year history of the ferry service. A large proportion of the ferryboat customers had always ridden the boats as much for pleasure as for transportation.

Each boat had a snack-food restaurant and a bar aboard. There are still many Contra Costans who can remember drinking a cold beer on the 20-minute ferry trip, standing on the stern feeding the seagulls, and listening to the hoarse hoot of the steam whistle, the propellers churning water, and--finally--to the boat creaking into its slip.

El Sobrante "Strip" Started in 1940s on San Pablo Road

El Sobrante is a Spanish name for the leftover land between ranchos. Two brothers, Victor and Juan Jose Castro, noted that most of the land in Contra Costa had been granted to various recipients over the years with the exception of El Sobrante. They applied for a grant and got it in 1841, but squatters soon took adverse possession and there were many squabbles over titles. The U.S. Land Commission awarded a few hundred acres to Castro heirs in 1882, with the bulk of the land going to others. Virtually all of it was used as farmland for more than a century. One exception was Oak Grove Park, which became a popular attraction for weekend picnickers who came via California and Nevada Railroad in the 1880s. The San Pablo Dam was completed in 1919, creating a useful and beautiful reservoir. The road along the reservoir -- from Richmond to Orinda -- was paved shortly after, making residential and commercial subdivisions possible. But the housing boom didn't start until World War II, when shipyard workers from Richmond started moving into El Sobrante. A commercial strip then started on San Pablo Dam Road, which by 1952 included Charles Morales's furniture store, a small Fry's market, a variety store, a barber shop, and Oliver's Hardware and Oliver's Chevron Station-- both owned by the same family. The station is shown in a 1947 photo, with Margaret and John Oliver and their two dogs, Boomer and Bing, out in front. This was a *service* station -- where they checked oil and tires and cleaned windshields -- and gas was 29 cents a gallon. Ah, the good old days!

El Cerrito Was Once Known for Dog Racing & Gambling; Reformers Made It into an All-American City

Politically separate, but geographically part of Greater Richmond, El Cerrito was originally called Rust, after William Rust, who came in 1888 and built a blacksmith shop and a home -- and later a hardware store and butcher shop -- along the dirt road between Oakland and Martinez, near the Castro Adobe. Prior to Rust's arrival Mr. and Mrs. John H. Davis had built Seven Mile House, a tavern and eating place, in the same area. They later converted a nearby barn into a popular dance hall. The dirt road became San Pablo Avenue and the town grew. In 1916 it was renamed El Cerrito ("Little Hill" in Spanish) after a nearby hill, which is actually inside the city limits of Albany. The most famous resident of El Cerrito at that time was Pierre ("French Pete") Allinio, who built and flew his own airplane in 1915 and three more planes in subsequent years. During the 1930s and early 1940s El Cerrito was best known for its wide-open gambling joints. Even the Castrro Adobe had become an illegal casino. Another less notorious feature of the town was the dog racing track. Dog racing was quite legal in those days. As a boy growing up in San Francisco I remember taking a ferryboat to El Cerrito with my grandparents to see the dog races, which were held at night under bright lights. Watching the swift greyhounds chase a mechanical rabbit around the track was exciting and a lot of fun. A reform group took over the city government in 1946 and drove the gamblers out. The state legislature banned dog racing. El Cerrito became a "City of Homes" and was declared an All-American City in 1954 by the National Municipal League and Look Magazine. A regional shopping center now occupies the places were the adobe and the dog track once were.

Kensington: A Hilly Enclave For Professors and Lawyers

Kensington, the East Bay's "Shangri-La," is a 900-acre triangular-shaped tract in the Berkeley hills, tucked between El Cerrito and Berkeley. If you lived in Kensington at a certain address on Arlington Avenue or Rugby Avenue, the house next door would be across the county line -- in Berkeley.

Kensington was sparsely settled before the Oakland Traction Company extended its service from downtown Berkeley up to Arlington Avenue and thence to the county line in 1911, thus prompting a series of real estate developments: "Berkeley Park," 1911; "Berkeley Highlands," 1913; "Berkeley Highland Terrace," 1914; "Berkeley Woods," 1920, and so on. Judging by these names, the inhabitants must have felt spiritually closer to Berkeley than to their other neighbor, El Cerrito. The hillside homes of Kensington, on crooked, narrow streets, have been occupied mostly by laureates, lawyers, professors, deans, and doctors. Daniel Elsberg, of Pentagon Papers fame, has been one of the residents. The most noticeable landmarks in the town are the Carmelite Monastery for Women, which communicates with outsiders through an opaque grill; the Blake Estate, a mansion once used as a residence of the Chancellor of U.C. Berkeley, and the Arlington Pharmacy, started in 1928 by Louis L. Stein Jr. and run by him for nearly 50 years. The pharmacy is shown as it appeared in 1950. Next door to it, in this photo, are a variety store, beauty parlor, barber, grocery, and dry cleaner -- the entire business district of Kensington.

Where Ramon Briones Killed a 1,000-Pound Bear

Rancho Briones Eventually Became a Park, As Did Other Wilderness Areas

The scratched-up photo of Bear Creek Falls shown at right was taken April 1, 1897, by Hunt Photographers of Martinez. The falls and creek were, and still are, a great scenic attraction. The falls were in the center of the 6,000-acre Rancho Briones. Bear Creek got its name from a 1,000-pound bear shot by Ramon Briones near these falls. This was the largest bear killed in Contra Costa County. Now part of Briones Regional Park, the falls are about two miles north of Orinda. Briones is a wilderness area, ideal for hiking, trail riding, and nature study. The park was frequented by hippie kids from nearby towns during the 1960s. The hippies have grown up long since and have become professional and business people and the park now has more conventional visitors. Contra Costa County (except for the far eastern section) voted to join the East Bay Regional Park District in 1962. The first park opened by the district in the county was Kennedy Grove, near El Sobrante. Briones was next, opening in 1967. Other major parks developed by the district in this county are as follows:

● Las Trampas and Little Hills--more than 3,000 acres with breathtaking views, in the San Ramon Valley.
● Brown's Island, near Pittsburg--once the site of **a bawdy house and a** haven for fishermen. The working girls are gone, but it's still a great place to fish.
● Black Diamond Mines, including the Nortonville townsite, with a museum and several old mining tunnels open to the public.

There are also a number of smaller parks developed by the district in Contra Costa, including Contra Loma, near Antioch; Diablo Foothills; Morgan Territory; a small part of the fabulous old Bishop Ranch; Sibley; Huckleberry; Redwood Canyon; Martinez Shoreline,; Antioch Shoreline, and Point Pinole, shown in the sketch at right.

175

Chapter 14

Crockett Was Named After Associate Justice Of Supreme Court

The town of Crockett was founded on part of the Rancho Cañada del Hambre by Thomas Edwards. A friend of Mr. Edwards, attorney J.B. Crockett of San Francisco, had acquired 1,800 acres of the land grant as a legal fee. In 1866 he persuaded Mr. Edwards to go into partnership with him to found a town on the land. Within a couple of years Mr. Edwards had gotten rid of squatters that had been living on the land and Mr. Crockett had become an associate justice on the California supreme court,. The town was finally laid out in 1881 and named after Justice Crockett. Another town, Valona, had already been started in 1877 on an adjoining parcel of Rancho Cañada by Dr. J.B. Strenzel. The photo at left shows Loring Avenue in Crockett about 10 years after the town was started. John Loring Heald had built a hotel—the Pinkerton House—in 1882 to house workers at his nearby factory, Heald Agricultural Works, which produced boilers, pumps, threshers, and other machinery. The hotel was renamed Crockett House about 1900. It is shown in the center of the picture. It has had many other names during the past 111 years and is still standing at the corner of Loring Avenue and Bay Street. Also shown in the photo, to the left of the hotel, are Paul Beda's store, the Arcade Hall, Davis's Store, a store owned by Thomas Edwards Jr., and the Odd Fellows Hall.

Crockett Firemen in 1911

Although Crockett and Valona were located side-by-side, there was intense rivalry between the two towns. Each town had its own fire department, movie theater, etc. The photo at left shows the Crockett firehouse at Winslow Avenue near Alhambra Avenue, with the volunteer fire fighters and their hose cart out in front. The man at the right, wearing a suit, is the fire chief, Tillie Arratta.

Carquinez Bridge
Under Construction

The Carquinez Bridge, linking Vallejo and Crockett, was nearly completed when this aerial photo was taken. Tugboats have pushed a cantilever section into position, ready to be hauled up by cables to become part of the bridge. The Rodeo-Vallejo ferry dock on the Solano side can be seen at right and the ferryboat *Issaquah* can be seen steaming along in the upper left. The American Toll Bridge Company was formed in 1921 and got a franchise to build the span. It has six piers, each the size of an 11-story building, which were constructed in the water and then pushed down through 40 feet of mud to bedrock, 135 feet below the surface. The bridge opened to traffic on May 21, 1927. The state took it over in 1940 and built a second twin bridge alongside it in 1958 to cope with increased traffic. The original bridge was listed in the Encyclopedia Americana as one of the notable cantilever bridges in the world.

A Spectacular View Of Crockett in the 1930s

A photographer climbed up in the hills on a clear day in the mid-1930s to shoot this remarkable panorama of Crockett, Carquinez Strait, and the hills of Solano County across the strait.

At left is the Carquinez Bridge, which is described more fully on another page.

The large buildings along the water's edge comprise the California and Hawaiian Sugar Refining Company. This enterprise began as the Starr Flour Mill, which was built in 1884, started production in 1891, and closed down during the financial panic of 1893. It became a sugar mill to refine beet sugar in 1897, but California farmers couldn't supply enough sugar beets at that time. The plant shut down in 1903, but was reborn as C & H in 1906 and has experienced substantial growth since, processing raw cane sugar from Hawaii.

Just to the right of the large smokestack is the Hotel Crockett, built by the original California Beet Sugar Company in 1898, then closed down for several years, and then reopened by C & H mainly to provide housing for its employees. The 170-room hotel was also the center of social events in Crockett for many years, most notably the annual Christmas party hosted by the sugar company, with a banquet and gifts for all employees and their families. As more and more employees bought homes, the need for the hotel diminished and it closed in 1941.

Shown across the strait (just above the big smokestack), nestled in a grove of trees, is Glen Cove, site of an ancient Indian shell mound.

In the lower right is the Carquinez Grammar School, built in 1924, with 24 classrooms, manual training room, music room, homemaking department, and other features. Just across the road is John Swett Union High School, built in 1927 and named after the world-famous educator who lived in nearby Martinez.

Today you wouldn't have to climb up in the hills to see a view like this; you can drive your car up Cummings Skyway, which was built in 1956.

Downtown View Of Valley Street

A delightful example of Americana is this view of Valley Street, Crockett, on a weekday afternoon in the early 1930s. You are looking north toward Winslow Street, with a C&H sugar refinery building in the background.

Customers' cars are parked in front of the little downtown stores, shaded by trees. The name of the street has been changed to Rolph Avenue, after George M. Rolph, president of C&H Sugar Company from 1926 to 1931.

The Rapid Growth and Sudden Decline of the Wheat Exporting Business

Starting in the mid-1870s the region around the Carquinez Strait became a center for shipping California wheat and other grains to ports all over the world. California wheat was drier than other varieties, which meant that it was less likely to spoil during long sea voyages. Also it absorbed more moisture during baking, producing heavier loaves of bread than other wheat. For these reasons it was in great demand by bakers. It was loaded onto schooners at the Carquinez docks and shipped around Cape Horn to New York, Boston, London, Liverpool, Dublin, Antwerp, Le Havre, Amsterdam, Hamburg, Algiers, and Rome. Also from the Carquinez docks, ships carried the golden grain across the Pacific to Tokyo, Hong Kong, Manila, and other ports.

Many farmers in Contra Costa and elsewhere in California were making fortunes growing wheat.

The Carquinez Strait region was chosen as a shipping point because it was easy to bring the grain here from the fields of the Sacramento and San Joaquin Valleys via river barges or trains. Plus there was deep fresh water for ocean-going vessels and an absence of toredos, the salt-water borers that eat pilings.

The first warehouse on the strait was built in 1876 by a coalition of Contra Costa Grange organizations at Eckley, a tiny community near Port Costa. Other warehouses and docks built subsequently included those of Eppinger and Company at Crockett; the California Wharf and Warehouse Company at Port Costa; Balfour Guthrie and Company at Benicia; Port Costa Warehouse and Dock Company at Port Costa; Nevada Warehouse and Dock Company at a location between Port Costa and Martinez, and Bernard Fernandez at Pinole.

The Eppinger warehouse was later called Banker's warehouse. It eventually became part of the C&H sugar refinery. Balfour Guthrie operated the California Wharf and Warehouse facility at Port Costa in addition to its own warehouse in Benicia. The Port Costa Warehouse and Dock Company later came into the ownership of the famed "grain king," George W. McNear.

The sensational growth of the wheat exporting business encouraged investors to speculate on the market. Frank Norris wrote a famous historical novel about the speculators, farmers, sailors, stevedores, and railroad men of the Carquinez Strait wheat business, "The Octopus," which has become a classic.

As an example of the magnitude of the business, in just one year, 1885, at one facility alone, the Nevada warehouse and dock, more than 300 thousand tons of grain were loaded into 161 ships.

James C. Flood and John W. Mackey, owners of the aforementioned facility, tried to corner the market in 1887-'88, using commission agent William Dresbach to do the buying.

Dresbach succeeded in driving wheat prices up to new highs but the money ran out and Flood and Mackey's bank lost $16 million. A vice president of the bank disappeared with a sachel full of money, leaving nobody to say exactly what happened.

Jim Fair was the next one to try to corner the market, in 1895, and also lost his fortune, followed later by George W. McNear, who also failed and became all but bankrupt.

In the early 1900s the grain business slowed to a near halt. Competing farmers in Oregon and in other countries had driven the prices down. The farmers in Contra Costa and elsewhere in California switched to more profitable vineyards and orchards.

California Wharf and Warehouse Company facility at Port Costa. It was operated by Balfour Guthrie

The *Solano*, World's Largest Ferryboat, Docked at Port Costa in 1913

The *Solano*, the world's largest ferryboat, could carry an entire freight train or several passenger trains. The big boat was built of wood in West Oakland in 1879. There were four railroad tracks on her deck and she was 420 feet long, somewhat longer than a football field. There were two huge 1,250-horsepower walking beam engines, each independently driving a sidewheel. The *Solano* carried more than 3,000 trains a year between Port Costa and Benicia from 1879 to 1930. The ferry service was a vital link in the nation's transcontinental rail system. The *Solano* is shown above docked at Port Costa in 1913, partially loaded with freight cars. Using four or five switch engines (nicknamed "boat goats") the loading crew could put an entire train aboard the *Solano* in a few minutes. The entire process of transporting a train from Port Costa to Benicia was accomplished in 30 or 40 minutes, including loading, trip time, and unloading. Engine foremen had to be careful to make the ferryboat "keel even," with the weight of the cars being approximately the same on both sides of the vessel. Port Costa was a boisterous place during the train and ferry era. There were some 14 bars in the tiny town, providing food and drink for the warehousemen, sailors, and railroaders who worked there. Some of the bars--and a hotel or two-- can be seen in the left background of the photo, along the waterfront. When local farmers brought wheat or other grains to Port Chicago for trans-shipment several thousand workers would also come to town: Irishmen, Mexicans, Italians, Portuguese, and Chinese. There were many riotous payday weekends at the waterfront, more often than not resulting in violence. It was not unusual for a body to be found floating in the straits. Railroad business increased over the years, requiring the contstruction of a second huge ferryboat, the *Contra Costa*, in 1914 to help carry the trains. This one was built of steel and was slightly bigger than the *Solano*. The busy times ended in Port Costa in 1930 when a railroad bridge was built between Martinez and Benicia. The *Solano* ended up in the mud flats near Antioch, serving as a breakwater and a fishing clubhouse. The steel hull of the *Contra Costa* was refashioned into three barges and the superstructure was dumped into deep water near the Carquinez Bridge. In 1950 the hulk was declared a menace to navigation and blown up. Port Costa is now a quiet little village with a few antique shops and eating places catering to visitors.

Courter's Store Was First Frame Building in Moraga Valley

WOODCUTTERS AND WAGON DRIVERS were the main customers of John Courter's general store and saloon, which opened in the spring of 1854—the first frame building in the Moraga Valley. In nearby Moraga Canyon (now called just *Canyon*), a horde of lumberjacks were busy demolishing 500 acres of huge redwood trees, each about as tall as a 14-story building. Tremendous logs, ten feet in diameter, were converted to lumber at several sawmills which had been erected near the logging operations. The lumber was carried away in wagons drawn by oxen along Canyon Road, which went right past Courter's place, near the present Larch Avenue intersection. As you might imagine, Courter's saloon was always full of thirsty lumberjacks and teamsters. These prosperous times did not last long, however. The last tree in Moraga Canyon was cut down in the fall of 1856. The store still had the local tenant farmers as customers, but there were no more lumbermen to patronize the saloon. Courter sold out in a few years. There were several changes of ownership, and then the store and saloon went out of business in 1872. The building was used as a hayloft for the next 50 years until its dilapidated remnant, shown in the picture, was torn down. Today there is no sign of Courter's place, not even an historical plaque, but the redwoods have come back. A new forest, only 137 years old, now stands in Canyon.

Chapter 15

Summit Saloon

Hansen's Hotel

Classen's Inn

The Old Saloons of Canyon

Canyon had started in the late 1840s as a lumbering center. There was a stand of redwoods there, thousands of years old, so tall that they were used as navigation points by ships entering San Francisco Bay. By the late 1850s the trees were gone, converted to lumber to build towns and cities in the Bay Area and elsewhere. The denuded hills of Canyon were then occupied by farms for the next 40 years. By the turn of the century the redwood trees had grown back. Many hikers, hunters, fishermen, and campers were visiting Canyon. Also the stage and wagon roads from Alamo and Lafayette to Oakland went through the area. To serve the outdoorsmen, travelers, and wagon drivers a number of saloons and small hotels opened in Canyon. Three of them are shown as they looked around the turn of the century. Hansen's Hotel had guest rooms upstairs and a saloon below. It was the Canyon stop for the stage coaches. Stage driver Henry Jones lived only a few hundred yards away from the hotel. He was known as Whispering Jones because of his booming voice. The Summit Saloon was on the old summit above Redwood Road and catered to some rather hardbitten characters. Classen's Inn was somewhat more genteel than the others. The Bottomley Saloon (not pictured here) featured cock fighting and gambling for entertainment. In 1906 Isaac Bottomley sold the place and started a new one, the Redwood Inn, about 200 yards below Hansen's Hotel.

The Redwood Grove in Canyon, 1940

IN THE LATE 1930s and early 1940s the community of Canyon consisted of about 150 homes nestled in the hills around a redwood grove. This is a picture of the grove in 1940. There were many picnic tables, used by residents and visitors. The building behind the trees was the Canyon Store (formerly the Redwood Inn), where people could buy groceries and other necessities such as kerosene for their stoves. (There were no natural gas lines in Canyon—and no streetlights, no sewers, and no sidewalks.) The store was also the lending library and the post office. For years it was run by Joe Knipe, who sold it to his son, who in turn sold it to the Canyon Store Trust, organized by a group of local residents. With its lumbering and dairy ranching days at an end, Canyon had become a summer resort area in the early 1900s. The Oakland and Antioch Railway came in 1913, bringing trainloads of picnickers from Oakland and San Francisco every summer. Then in the 1920s many summer home subdivisions were started. During the Depression people started living in Canyon year-round. After World War II much Canyon land was bought up by East Bay Municipal Utilities District as a watershed, and the number of homes steadily declined. In the late 1960s and early 1970s "weekend hippies" from neighboring towns gathered regularly in the redwood grove to the consternation of Canyon residents. The Canyon Store and post office was destroyed by an explosion and fire caused by a leaking Shell gasoline pipeline. The store was never rebuilt. The post office was housed in a trailer till 1984, when a new post office was built.

Moraga Barn Was Never A Barn

THE MORAGA BARN, a nearly square frame building with a hip roof, was built in 1914 by Robert N. Burgess. It was intended to be a hotel, with five bedrooms on the top floor, each with a washstand and shower. The main floor lobby was two stories high. Later the upper floor was converted to an apartment and a middle floor was added. Tracks of the Sacramento - Northern Railway ran in front of the building, parallel with the road. John Fleuti bought the building in 1915 and turned it into a general store. In 1921 his daughter Helen (Mrs. John Smart) moved from Oakland to Moraga to manage the store. It was called Moraga Mercantile. The stock included groceries, meat, dry goods, hardware, and drugs. The customers were mostly the grain, hay, and dairy ranchers of Moraga Valley. The store was the voter registration office, post office, and telephone exchange—and it even had a soda fountain. After the end of Prohibition in 1933, Moraga

Mercantile began serving beer, and then other alcoholic beverages. The grocery and drug counters were moved to one side, until the demand for them ceased entirely. The place became known as the Moraga Bar, until 1935, when a new state law prohibited the use of the name "bar." An "N" was added to the sign outside and the Moraga Bar became the Moraga Barn. The place is shown in the center of this late 1950s aerial photo. The railroad tracks had been torn up in 1957. Just to the left of the building you can see the urns on Munster Drive (now Country Club Drive), which were the beginnings of an unsuccessful subdivision planned by the Moraga Company in 1913. To the right is the Moraga Post Office building, constructed in 1954, now used as a dental office. Today the old ranches are gone; the Moraga Barn is flanked by shopping centers and surrounded by ranch-style homes.

Saint Mary's Groundbreaking Ceremony, 1927

GROUNDBREAKING CEREMONIES for Saint Mary's College were held May, 15, 1927, attended by some 5,000 people, many of whom came on four special trains from Oakland to the San Francisco-Sacramento Railway station on the edge of the campus site. (The railroad was later called the Sacramento Northern.) The picture shows the speakers platform and some of the spectators. The top of the hill with the "M" is now marked by a cross. Archbishop Edward Hanna turned the first shovelful of earth and bestowed a blessing. Following the groundbreaking, there was a graduation exercise for a class of 23 students from the college's Oakland campus. Saint Mary's College was founded as a parish school in San Francisco in 1863. It became a college in 1868, directed by the Christian Brothers. In 1889 it moved to Oakland. Years later, needing space to expand, the college accepted the offer of 100 acres in Moraga from the Moraga Company and purchased 300 acres more. Thirteen buildings to accomodate 1,000 students were included in the original $3 million Moraga campus, which was first occupied in 1928.

Saint Mary's Pre-Flight School Trained Navy Pilots

SAINT MARY'S COLLEGE went to war seven weeks after Pearl Harbor. On February 27, 1942, Secretary of the Navy Frank Knox accepted the college's offer of its campus, which was selected for pre-flight training. The first contingent of future Navy fliers, 300 cadets, arrived at Saint Mary's the following June. They were called 90-day wonders because the rigorous training course lasted three short months. Daily runs over an obstacle course, technical studies, and marching in formation were included in the curriculum. The photo shows a class of cadets marching past the landmark chapel at Saint Mary's. The Navy took over many campus buildings and built many additional temporary structures—barracks, gymnasia, a mess hall, field house, infirmary, and a rifle range. The quiet serenity of the college gave way to the staccato of construction. The civilian student body was reduced to 250 students because of the draft. Saint Mary's Pre-Flight School trained approximately 15,000 recruits in Moraga from June 1, 1942, until it was decommisioned on June 30, 1946. Football continued at the college during the war, as the pre-flight school had stellar All-American recruits, who had been scouted from various universities to publicize the Navy's pre-flight program. One of the all-time greats at Saint Mary's then was Frankie Albert, formerly with Stanford, the golden arm of the T-formation, who was graduated from the pre-flight school to serve as a lieutenant in the Navy. After the war he became captain of the first Forty Niners team. One of the football coaches at Saint Mary's Pre-Flight was Gerald Ford, who later became President of the United States.

Railroad Was Orinda's Link with the World

THE CALIFORNIA AND NEVADA Railroad was a narrow-gauge line with wood-burning locomotives. It operated all through the 1890s, going from Emeryville through Berkeley, San Pablo, and along San Pablo Creek through the present site of El Sobrante to Orinda Park Station and thence to Bryant Station, which was located near the site occupied by the Orinda Theatre many years later. The railroad was planned to go all the way to Utah, but never got farther east than Contra Costa County. It carried hay, grain, and produce to the markets in Oakland and brought back supplies and hardware to Contra Costa farmers. It also carried passengers from Oakland to enjoy holidays at the various recreation places in Contra Costa. There were picnic spots and/or swimming holes along San Pablo Creek, at Thode Oak Grove, at the Clancy Ranch, at the Symmons Ranch in Orinda Park, and near Bryant Station. This 1894 picture shows a train stopped on one of the trestles near the present site of Orinda. If you look closely you can see a crowd of picnickers standing on a flat car and the engineer and fireman standing in the locomotive, all posing for this photo. The railroad was purchased by Santa Fe in 1899 and the line to Bryant Station was abandoned soon after.

Early Tunnel Shortened Journey to Oakland

BACK IN THE 1880s it took more than two hours to go by stage coach from Lafayette to Oakland. Going over the top of the hills between Alameda and Contra Costa Counties was the worst part of the journey. There were many accidents, some fatal, when horse-drawn vehicles got our of control on the steep slopes and crashed into each other. A tunnel had been talked about since the 1860s, but nothing was done about it until the late 1870s, when the Oakland and Contra Costa Tunnel Company built the Kennedy Toll Road and dug out 100 feet of tunnel on the Contra Costa side and 200 feet on the Alameda County side. However, the project was abandoned when the firm ran out of money. In the 1890s another campaign was started to get the tunnel completed, with leading citizens contributing part of the funds, along with the two county governments. After years of planning, fund raising, and digging, the 1,100-foot tunnel was finally opened in 1903. It was 320 feet lower than the top of Summit Road, thereby cutting out the steepest part of the climb over the hills. The tunnel was narrow and dark, so wagon drivers lit up newspapers when entering to signal those at the other end to wait. This picture was taken about 1918. The flag-decorated cars must have been part of a special procession—but who was that lady at the other side of the road?

190

Canary Cottage Served Travelers On Tunnel Road

TRACES OF SNOW were slowly melting on the roofs of cars parked in front of the Canary Cottage Roadhouse, on Tunnel Road, near the east portal of the old high-level single-bore tunnel that connected Contra Costa with Oakland (until a new low-level tunnel was built in 1937). The old tunnel was narrow (just one lane) and the road was steep and winding. The date was January 29, 1922. A brisk snowfall had covered the cottage roof and the road. It was the first snow in eight years and the heaviest since 1882. The roadhouse had been serving travelers about a dozen years, providing food and gasoline. It had been owned by Basil A. Perry, who sold it in 1918 to Frank Enos and his wife Ruth, who

gave it the name Canary Cottage. When the nearby tunnel got equipped with electric lights in 1919, Mr. Enos made a deal with the power company—for him to replace burnt out light bulbs in the tunnel in exchange for free electricity for his roadhouse. The Enoses left Canary Cottage later in 1922 to move to Orinda, where they built another small restaurant and gas station which they called the White Swan. Located just past the bridge at the north end of Orinda Village, it was the first structure there other than a barn a little farther down the road, which was later known as Casa Verana. Nobody has recorded why the Enoses named their little restaurants·after birds.

Tree Planting Day at Orinda School— March 7, 1925

MARCH 7, 1925, was Tree Planting Day at the new Orinda School. Each child planted a tree, with some adult help. One of the school trustees, George A. Brockhurst, had previously gone over the ground with a horse-drawn grader. The school was the first built by the Orinda Union School District, which had been formed by consolidating the former Orinda Park and Moraga School Districts in 1923. The new district abandoned the Orinda Park schoolhouse (which had been built in 1882) as soon as this new school was in operation. Maude Woodin, who had been a teacher at Orinda Park School, became the first principal of the new school. It had been built with funds from a $22,000 bond issue, which passed in 1924 with 23 votes in favor, none against. It had two classrooms and an auditorium. The school was dedicated on April 11, 1925. Trustee Edward I. deLaveaga gave the main address at the formal ceremonies, which were attended by citizens from all over the county. In 1939 the school was enlarged and rebuilt, with a new playground, six classrooms, an auditorium, kitchen, two playrooms, principal's office, and library.

Miss Graham's Riding Class at Orinda Country Club

HERE IS MISS GRAHAM'S riding class on Camino Sobrante in 1925, with the nearly completed clubhouse of the Orinda Country Club in the background. Miss Graham (Mrs. Philip R. Donaldson) had stables and a riding academy in Orinda Village. Her husband was one of the early-day chiefs of the Orinda Volunteer Fire Department, and then a sheriff's deputy from 1935 to 1962. The country club was promoted by Edward I. deLaveaga, who had started subdividing his Orinda land in 1921. The country club included the clubhouse, a golf course, and a swimming pool—occupying 159 acres next to Lake Cascade, which had been formed by the construction of a dam. The clubhouse, which cost $214,000, opened in September 1925. The 18-hole golf course was laid out by William Watson, famed course designer. It was 6,315 yards long, with a par of 72. The swimming pool, with a Spanish-style bath house, was and is unique. A waterfall goes into a small pool (a copy of the "Blue Hole" of the Mokelumne River) and from there spills into the large swimming pool. The Orinda Country Club hosted its first major golf tournament in April 1928. It was won by 17-year-old Lawson Little. Ralph Longo was the first club pro, followed in 1942 by Pat Patten.

Low-Level Tunnel Opened Contra Costa County to Commuters

A NEW ERA of suburban residential development started with the opening of the Broadway Low-Level Tunnel on December 5, 1937. First there were ceremonies at the Oakland side of the tunnel, which included fireworks and Army planes and pigeons flying overhead. Then the final dedication was held at the Orinda side. With afternoon shadows darkening the hills, a huge crowd listened to speeches by Governor Frank Merriam, Supervisor W. J. Buchanan, and others. During the speeches cars were all lined up at the tunnel entrances. Shortly after this photo was taken the people got into their cars, the governor gave a signal, there was another burst of fireworks, and the traffic started through, bumper-to-bumper for miles. There were two bores in the tunnel, one for east-bound traffic, the other for west-bound. A special joint highway district had been formed in 1928 to accomplish the project, which cost $11 million. Thomas F. Caldecott, president of the district, was honored later when the tunnel was rededicated bearing his name. A third bore was made in 1964 to cope with increased traffic.

Orinda Theatre—An Art Deco Landmark

In November 1948, when this picture was taken, traffic signals had just been installed at Orinda Crossroads. The commercial district then included the Moraga Hills Pharmacy (left), the Orinda Theatre, the Orinda Sweet Shop, and a Flying "A" Associated gas station. There was no freeway then. That's the main highway, with the two-tone car heading east, toward Lafayette. Commuters had already discovered Contra Costa. The post-war building boom was just beginning. The theatre had been built by Donald Rheem in 1941. The architect was Alexander A. Cantin, who had collaborated on San Francisco's famed telephone building. The decorator was Anthony B. Heinsbergen, who had done the interiors of most San Francisco first-run movie houses. The art deco curves and ornamentation of the exterior made the theatre an outstanding landmark for half a century. Heinsber-

gen's interior is considered to be a masterpiece of its kind, featuring surrealistic scenes of god-like figures representing earth, fire, air, and water. The theatre was the center of a national controversy in 1984, when it was scheduled to be torn down. That idea was opposed by the National Trust for Historic Preservation, the Art Deco Society, the Architectural Heritage Association, the Society of Architectural Historians, the California State Historical Resources Commission, and last—but not least—the Friends of the Orinda Theatre, who gathered 22,000 signatures from local citizens on a petition demanding preservation of the theatre. After months of negotiations a compromise was reached and the theatre was preserved amid some additions that improved the owner's bottom line, and may actually have improved the esthetics of the property, in the opinion of many.

Chapter 16

A Hotel on Mount Diablo in 1874

A GREAT IDEA—probably before its time—was the Mountain House. It was an elegant little 16-room hotel, built near a spring above Pine Canyon, about a mile from the summit of Mount Diablo. Joseph H. Hall, an ingenious Yankee from New Hampshire, built Mountain House in 1874 and was instrumental in getting two roads built—one from Ygnacio Valley and one from Danville—which met in front of the hotel. Daily stage coaches brought guests from Martinez, Pacheco, and Concord and from Oakland, Hayward, and Danville. The rather fuzzy picture (the only one we could find) shows one of the stages arriving in front of the hotel. Mountain House had a large dining room where guests could enjoy the food and the view. There was also an observation platform and telescope for use of the guests. Seeing dawn or sunset from Mountain House must have been awe-inspiring. The register of the hotel showed names of people from all over the world. Many couples were married there. Mountain House was successful for a number of years, but problems arose. Most of the mountain was then privately owned, mostly by ranchers, who objected to sightseers overrunning their land. The ranchers claimed that careless hotel guests had caused fires, which ruined pasture lands. The ranchers petitioned the Board of Supervisors to close the mountain roads. The petition was granted; gates and fences kept the public out. The hotel was burned down. It wasn't till years later that the mountain was again open to the public—and nobody has yet rebuilt the elegant little hotel.

Scenic Boulevard Brought Thousands Of Sightseers to the Top of Mount Diablo

Thousands -- possibly millions -- of people have climbed to the summit of Mount Diablo to see spectacular panoramas of a larger area of land and water than can be seen from any peak in the world, except Mount Kilimanjaro in Africa. On a clear day it is possible to see 35 of California's 58 counties!

In May 1874 two roads to the summit were opened, one from Ygnacio Valley through Pine Canyon and the other from Danville. Stage coaches ran twice daily from Oakland and Martinez to the mountain top.

However, in 1891 ranch owners on the mountain, irked by the traffic, succeeded in having the roads closed. It wasn't till 1915 that Mount Diablo Scenic Boulevard, 23 miles long, was opened to the public. Horse-drawn wagons and motor-driven jitneys did a brisk trade taking sightseers up the mountain.

The photo shows the toll gate on the Danville side of the mountain. The Anderson family of Tassajara stopped to have their picture taken in November 1917 with their new seven-passenger Jeffery touring car. Toll rates were as follows: auto with two passengers, $1; two-horse vehicle, $1.50; four-horse vehicle, $2; individual person, 25 cents; horse or cow, 10 cents, and sheep, 2-1/2 cents each.

Mount Diablo Was Dedicated as a California State Park in 1921

The crowd shown in this photo, taken by Lancaster Studios of Martinez, assembled at the top of Mount Diablo on Sunday, June 19, 1921. Following is the text of a news story that appeared the next day on the front page of the *Martinez Daily Standard*:

All sections of Contra Costa joined hands on Sunday in a great celebration on Mount Diablo—joined in celebrating an event that will live long in after years as the great Mount Diablo State Park is developed.

The affair was handled by a committee from Mount Diablo Parlor of Native Sons of the Golden West, Martinez, supplemented by a number of enterprising and energetic citizens. The Native Sons initiated the movement for the celebration because the parlor in Martinez is named after the historic old mountain.

Attorney James F. Hoey presided as chairman at exercises held in the morning at the base of the mountain and in the afternoon at the peak. Addresses were made by District Attorney A.B. Tinning, Dr. Victory A. Derrick, grand president of the Native Daughters; Lieutenant Governor C.C. Young, Attorney Charles L. McEnerney of San Francisco, Senator Will Sharkey, and Judge A.S. Ormsby. Music was furnished by the Martinez band. A pleasant feature of the affair was the program of the Martinez Choral Society. The amphitheatre affords a splendid site for outdoor programs. The voices of the speakers carried well in the open air; the band music was re-echoed through the canyons and was

heard miles away. The voices of the choral society floated out over the audience in perfect harmony and the great crowd was captivated by the beautiful selections and well trained voices. Mrs. William H. Hanlon, in a charming soprano voice that has made her a popular favorite in the bay cities, led the chorus of voices. The members of the society won high compliments for their program and their presence proved a most attractive and pleasant feature of the celebration.

At the conclusion of the program in the amphitheatre lunches were hastily disposed of and the crowd started for the top, nearly 4,000 feet above sea level. The boulevard is in good condition and the journey was made with ease. Probably for the first time in its history Mount Diablo on Sunday held a piano on its highest point. The piano was taken up on a truck and surrounding it the choral society rendered its selections. As the band played the "Star Spangled Banner" and the choral society sang the song, the American flag and the bear flag were raised on the pole erected five years ago by the Native Sons. The scene was truly remarkable as the crowd stood with heads bared. Brief addresses by Judge Ormsby and Attorneys Hoey and McEnerney completed the program.

From the top of the mountain the crowd looked out over the Golden Gate and many counties of California. The local committee is grateful for the support given by the people of Danville: Ralph Harrison, Charles Goold, Reed Eddy, J. Adam Freitas, and Ben Read, and the members of the Diablo Club.

3849 FEET ABOVE SEA LEVEL
DEDICATION OF MT. DIABLO STATE PARK
BY NATIVE SONS JUNE 19TH 1921.

The Great California DELTA

Sketch Map Shows Principal Communities, Islands, Waterways, and Highways

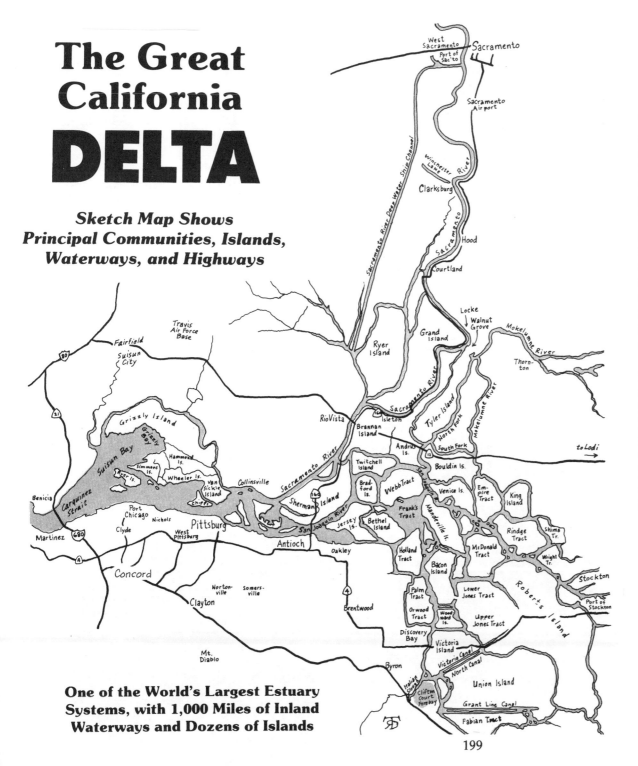

West Sacramento
Sacramento
Port of Sac'to
Sacramento Airport
Sacramento River Deep Water Ship Channel
Winchester Lake
Sacramento River
Clarksburg
Hood
Courtland
Locke
Walnut Grove
Mokelumne River
Thornton
Travis Air Force Base
Fairfield
Suisun City
Grand Island
Ryer Island
Tyler Island
North Fork
Mokelumne River
South Fork
to Lodi
Grizzly Island
Grizzly Bay
Suisun Bay
Hammond Is.
Simmons Is.
Ryer Is.
Wheeler Is.
Van Sickle Island
Chipps
RioVista
Isleton
Brannan Island
Andrus Is.
Twitchell Island
Bouldin Is.
Bradford Is.
Webb Tract
Venice Is.
Empire Tract
King Island
Benicia
Carquinez Strait
Collinsville
Sacramento River
Sherman Island
Franks Tract
Mandeville Is.
Rindge Tract
Shima Tr.
Port Chicago
Nichols
Pittsburg
San Joaquin River
Jersey Is.
Bethel Island
McDonald Tract
Wright Tr.
Martinez
Clyde
West Pittsburg
Antioch
Oakley
Holland Tract
Bacon Island
Stockton
Port of Stockton
Concord
Norton-ville
Somers-ville
Palm Tract
Lower Jones Tract
Roberts Island
Clayton
Brentwood
Orwood Tract
Woodward Is.
Upper Jones Tract
Mt. Diablo
Discovery Bay
Victoria Island
Byron
Victoria Canal
North Canal
Union Island
Clifton Court Forebay
Italian Slough
Grant Line Canal
Fabian Tract

One of the World's Largest Estuary Systems, with 1,000 Miles of Inland Waterways and Dozens of Islands

199

Delta Region of Contra Costa Famed for Water Sports, Fishing, Farming

The California Delta is one of the world's largest estuary systems. The sketch-map by the author shows the extent of the system, reaching north to Sacramento and south past Stockton. It is the place where three rivers--the Sacramento, San Joaquin, and Mokelumne--come together on their way to San Francisco Bay and the Pacific Ocean. The Delta region extends through four counties--Contra Costa, Solano, Sacramento, and San Joaquin. The area was originally swamps and marshes. A system of levees, started in the 1860s, has transformed the Delta into a network of rivers, sloughs, and islands. There are more than 1,000 miles of waterways, most of them navigable. Some are deep enough for ocean-going ships to reach the ports of Stockton and Sacramento.

The islands range from tiny patches of land to 20,000 acres. Included within the boundaries of Contra Costa County are a number of the larger islands: Bethel, Bradford, Jersey, Coney, Quimby, and Holland Islands, and Franks, Webb, Veale, Palm, and Orwood Tracts. Boating and fishing enthusiasts throng to this area, especially to Bethel Island and Franks Tract. The fertile soil of the islands has produced huge crops of asparagus, potatoes, celery, barley, sunflowers, safflower, and tomatoes.

Growing Potatoes
In the Delta, 1924

The photo shows a mechanical potato digger, powered with a small gas engine, operating on one of the Delta islands in 1924. Horses were used in this instance, but diggers like this one were also pulled by small tractors. Asparagus, potatoes, and celery were the main crops in the Delta in the late 1800s and early 1900s. By the 1950s the emphasis had shifted to corn, grain, barley, tomatoes, sunflowers, and safflower. Many of the islands in the Delta also provided pasture for beef and dairy cattle.

The Bradford-Jersey Island
Auto Ferry, 1956

The little ferry boat *Victory II* is shown leaving Bradford Island in 1956, heading across False River (one of the sloughs of the Delta) toward Jersey Island. The *Victory II*, with a capacity of six automobiles, has been provided by the county as a free service in lieu of bridges, also linking Webb Tract.

Jersey Island was reclaimed from marshland in 1860. The largest single field of celery ever planted, 1600 acres, was harvested there in 1918. The island once had a hotel, general store, blacksmith shop, barley mill, schoolhouse, post office, and a riverboat fueling station, operated by Standard Oil.

Bradford Island was reclaimed in the early 1900s by John C. Franks and several associates. The island once produced asparagus, which was packed there and brought to Antioch for shipment.

Webb Tract is the largest island in East County. Sugar beets, corn, and barley have been grown there.

Delta Riverboat Race Was Highlight of 1935 Movie

THERE WAS a time when riverboats carried passengers and freight up and down the Delta. There were regular runs between San Francisco and both Stockton and Sacramento, with stops at Pittsburg, Antioch, and other riverports. Steamboats were plying these waters even before California became a state, bringing '49ers to the gold fields. By the late 1800s riverboats had become large pleasure craft, with bars, restaurants, dance floors, and luxurious cabins—each taking hundreds of passengers on leisurely cruises to their destinations. However, by the 1920s the

boats had virtually disappeared, unable to compete with railroads and highways. The riverboats had their last moments of glory in a Will Rogers movie, "Steamboat Round the Bend," made in 1935. The photo shows (left to right) the *T.C. Walker*, *Fort Sutter*, *Cherokee Leader*, and *Pride of the River* at the start of a riverboat race that was a dramatic climax of the film. Incidentally, that was but one of several movies made in the Delta region, another notable one being "Cool Hand Luke," starring Paul Newman, in 1967.

There Is No End to the Story

History is unfinished business, especially the history we have recounted here, which for the most part ends in 1960. In fact, there have been more changes in our way of life in the 30-some-odd years since 1960 than in the 170 years before—and there were more changes in those 170 years than in several thousand years before that era.

Change is moving at an accelerated pace, mostly for the better, but I would ruin my reputation as a critic if I didn't point out some of the changes for the worse, such as those cereal-box-design buildings the Bank of America put up in Concord. One of the employees of BofA thought I was kidding when I said, "There goes the neighborhood!"

The wonderful old Bishop Ranch is getting overrun with office buildings, and the last farm in Pleasant Hill became a housing development a few years ago,

and Jim O'Hara's old orchards in Oakley are being subdivided. If John Muir came back for a visit he would be appalled. A lot of people moved to Contra Costa to enjoy the beautiful countryside; if many more move here there won't be any countryside.

> ## We must always have old memories and young hopes.
>
> —Message found in a fortune cookie
> at the Sun and Moon Restaurant
> in Concord

Another thing that's wrong with Contra Costa is the Naval Weapons Station. With its underground nuclear weapons, and its bomb-laden trucks driving on city streets, and its munition ships plying Carquinez Strait, the place is a menace. As Will Perry, the former county disaster chief, said, "If one of those munition ships runs into an oil tanker, we can kiss our assets goodbye."

However, mostly the county is in good shape. It's a beautiful spring day as I write these words. God's in His heaven and, mostly, all's right with the world.

Closing on a positive note, one has to applaud the preservation of historical buildings, artifacts, and photos in recent years. Especially notable are the Borges Ranch and Shadelands Ranch in Walnut Creek, the history center in Pleasant Hill, and historical museums in Martinez, Pittsburg, and Richmond.

About the Authors

The principal author of this work is known as Bob Tatam to most of his friends, but decided to use his full name on the title page because, as he puts it, "Would *Treasure Island* still be a classic if it were written by Bob Stevenson?"

Robert and Emily Tatam

Mr. Tatam has worked as a reporter, editor, advertising salesman, and publisher on various newspapers, including the *Walnut Kernel, San Francisco Chronicle, Pittsburg Post-Dispatch,* and *Concord Transcript.* He was editor and pub-

lisher of the *Diablo Beacon* in the late 1960s. In partnership with his late wife, Emily, he published community newspapers in Concord, Martinez, Moraga, and Alamo. He has also worked at various times as a real estate agent, department store manager, and journeyman machinist. He wrote a book on crime prevention which won high praise from the attorney general's office in Washington and is now working as a free-lance writer, artist, and designer with his partner and fiancée, Loicy Myers.

Emily Tatam was a civic leader, writer, and publisher. She served terms as vice president of the Contra Costa Council for Responsible Parenthood and the Adult Advisory Board to the Concord Youth Council. Giants Day in Concord, which she founded

in 1974, is still celebrated at the Concord Pavilion. She was founding sponsor of the High School Students' Center Committee, the largest youth organization in the county, which presented rock concerts and coffee house entertainment in the 1960s and '70s.

Earl Berkeley was the quintessential newspaper man. He worked for the *San Francisco Chronicle, San Francisco Progress, Antioch Ledger,* and many, many other papers. In the early 1950s he was the general manager of the *Contra Costa Times.*

As a free-lance writer, Paul Anderson wrote an outstanding biography of William Parmer Fuller, the man who founded the big paint company. Mr. Anderson and his wife were partners with the Tatams publishing the *Contra Costa Home Hunters Guide.*

FRONT COVER DESIGN: *Adapted from the pattern of a bandana like the ones worn by* vaqueros *(cowboys) who rode their horses over the hills and valleys of Contra Costa in the 1840s and '50s. Those were the days before American farmers came and fenced the rangelands. Those original bandanas were made in India. (Now they are made in the U.S. and many other places, still decorated with the old Indian patterns.) The photo shows Noah Adams, owner of a lumber company in Concord, at the wheel of his new car in 1911. The cover design thus symbolizes the contrast between a very old lifestyle and the start of the automotive age.* TITLE PAGE: *Martinez school bus, 1910.*